THE BIBLE:
WHAT'S THE POINT?

Scripture taken from the HOLY BIBLE, NEW INTERNATIONAL VERSION. Copyright © 1973, 1978, 1984 International Bible Society. Used by permission of Zondervan Bible Publishers.

Published by CLC Publishing, LLC.
Mustang, OK 73064

Printed in the United States of America

Book Design by Shannon Whittington

ISBN: 9781723837593

Non-Fiction

Christian

The Bible:
What's the Point?

Deanna Priebe

Thank you to those who have inspired in me a love for God's word.

J. D. and Kay
Kent
Keith
Nelmarie
Estellene

Table of Contents

INTRODUCTION

I am excited that you, in particular, have picked up this book to read. I love the story of the Bible and believe that it is very exciting. It is riveting in places. It is life-changing and convicting. It is reassuring. God's love for people is often overwhelming. Sometimes as you read, it's hard to understand why God does what he does. The story, at times, may seem to drag on slowly. Some places can even seem confusing. I hope this book will help you understand some of the story lines that are found in the Bible, so that when you pick up the Bible you will find it inviting as well as easier to read and understand.

The Bible is divided into two parts. It contains the Old Testament and then the New Testament. The Old Testament is about what happens from "the beginning"—before time began—until shortly before Jesus' conception and birth. The New Testament picks up the story from the conception and birth of Jesus and follows it through Jesus' life, death, burial, resurrection from the dead and ascension into heaven. It tells about the beginning of the church and follows the teaching and actions of Jesus' followers who were still on earth after Jesus ascended into heaven. Even though the Bible has been divided into two parts, the Old and New Testaments are part of one continuing story.

Not all of the Bible is written in chronological order. That can make it hard for readers to understand what is happening and why it is happening—how it fits into the overall context and timeline of the Bible.

This book begins with a very brief telling of the story of the Bible. Each successive chapter tells the story again, from a different perspective, or in light of a particular theme, focusing on different parts of the overall story. Some events are repeated in several chapters of the book, but the focus may be on different aspects of the story. I encourage you to read each chapter or story, then go back and look up any references you want to explore further. The last chapter addresses the question:

What Does This Have To Do With Me?

I pray that each time you read the story of the Bible, you will see more and more of God, of his love and of his will for people. This book has been written to help you begin to see that. I pray also that this book will only whet your appetite. When you have finished it, open the pages of God's book, the Bible. There you will find the story in its entirety.

Now… Enjoy your reading and the story of an awesomely magnificent and loving God!

A STORY SO SIMPLE

The Bible begins with the story of creation. It says that in six days, God created the world. He made light, and there was day and night. He made the sky and separated the water from the land. He made plants, and he made the sun and moon. He made creatures in the sea and in the sky. On the sixth day, God made animals, and then he made man in his own image. From man, God made woman. And then on the seventh day, God rested from the work he had done.

God placed the man and woman in the Garden of Eden where he provided all they needed. He walked about in the garden and talked with them. There was only one thing he told them not to do. They could not eat from one tree in the garden—the tree of knowledge of good and evil. God told them that if they ate from it they would die.

One day, a serpent tempted the woman, Eve, to eat from that tree and to be more like God, knowing good from evil. She listened and gave in to the temptation, and then Adam also ate from the tree. When they disobeyed God, they sinned.

Sin and death had entered the world and now stood between God and the people he had created in his image. Adam and Eve suffered consequences for their disobedience. God loved them, and he did what he had said he would do. He banished them from the garden, and eventually they would die.

God already had a plan to restore the relationship between him and the people he had created. He wanted people to be obedient to him, and he wanted to bless the people whom he had created. God said that someday One would crush the tempter's head, the tempter who had enticed Adam and Eve to sin. This was part of God's plan.

Once they were outside the garden, Adam and Eve had children and grandchildren. The number of men and women on the earth increased. Sin and wickedness also increased. When God saw how great the wickedness had become, he grieved that he had made people and decided to destroy them and all life on the earth.

There was one righteous man who found favor with God, though. His name was Noah. God wanted to save him and his family, so he told Noah to build an ark, a big boat. You see, God was going to flood the entire earth. It was in the ark that Noah's family, along with some of the animals, would be saved. Noah obeyed God and built the ark. He, his family and the animals went into the ark, and God closed the door.

It rained and rained, water came up from under the ground, and a flood covered the earth. After the floodwaters were gone, Noah and his family came out of the ark. They were fruitful and multiplied. And people were eventually scattered over the earth.

One day, God spoke to a man named Abram and wanted him to leave his people and the place where he was living. He said he would show Abram where to go and that he would bless Abram and his descendants. God planned to give Abram's descendents a land of their own. He even said all people on earth would be blessed through Abram. This was also part of God's plan.

God changed Abram's name to Abraham. Abraham's wife gave birth to a son whom they named Isaac. Then Isaac had twin sons, Jacob and Esau. Jacob had twelve sons. God changed Jacob's name to Israel, and Abraham's descendants through Jacob became known as the Israelites. God blessed Abraham's sons, his grandsons and his great-grandsons. True to his word, God was blessing Abraham's descendents.

Jacob favored his son, Joseph, and his other sons knew it. Because of their jealousy, they plotted together and ended up selling their brother, Joseph, to some traders who passed by. Joseph ended up being taken to Egypt. His experience there included being given much responsibility and trust, as well as eventually being thrown into prison because of a false accusation.

Pharaoh, the Egyptian king, had two dreams, and no one could tell him what he had dreamed or what the dreams meant. He found out that, while in prison, Joseph had interpreted other dreams. He had Joseph brought to him from prison, and Joseph was enabled by God to do what others could not do. He told Pharaoh what the dreams were and what they meant. There would be seven years of plenty in the land followed by seven years of famine. Because of Joseph's wisdom, Pharaoh chose him to prepare the country for the famine.

When the famine came, Joseph's brothers went to Egypt to look for food. The second time they went there for food, they were reunited with Joseph. The brothers were afraid, but Joseph assured them that what had happened was God's doing. God had sent him to Egypt for a purpose. So Jacob, his sons and their families all ended up moving to Egypt where Joseph could provide for them.

After living there a long time, one of the Pharaohs realized how numerous the Israelite people had become, and he enslaved them. The Egyptians were very cruel to them, and eventually the people cried out to God. God remembered the promises he had made to Abraham and therefore paid attention to their cries for help.

In response to his people's cry for help, God called a man named Moses to deliver his people from slavery in Egypt. The Pharaoh, or king, was a stubborn man, and God had to inflict plagues on Egypt before the Pharaoh would let

God's people go. Finally, he said they could go, and Moses led them away from there. When they came to the Red Sea, God parted the waters so his people could cross safely on dry land. The Egyptians followed the Israelites, but God caused the waters to close on them, and they drowned.

When the Israelites reached Mount Sinai, God gave Moses the Ten Commandments and the rest of his law for his people. He told them that if they fully obeyed his word, he would bless them, and they would be his treasured possession. Although the whole earth is his, he said the Israelites would be a holy nation. But if they disobeyed his word, they would experience many disasters.

God loved his people and wanted to bless them. He also wanted them to be obedient to him. He had told Abraham that he would give his descendents a land of their own, and so he began leading them to that promised land. When they got there, the people didn't trust God. Because of that, God made them wander in the desert for about forty years. During that time, the people continued to doubt and disobey God. Moses reminded them that if they would obey God, he would bless them. He also reminded them that there would be unpleasant and painful consequences if they did not obey. At the end of the forty years, the generation of people who had not trusted God at the entrance to the promised land had died. Only Moses and two other men from that generation of people were still alive. They had not doubted God. Moses had sinned in the desert, though, and did not get to enter the promised land. The other two men, Joshua and Caleb, did enter the land God had promised.

Moses died, and Joshua became the new leader of God's people. He led them into the promised land. Joshua reminded the people, as Moses had, about the numerous blessings they would receive if they were obedient to God and about the consequences that would follow their disobedience. He told them to choose who they would obey. If they chose God, they were to get rid of the false gods and were to serve the Lord God faithfully. The choice was theirs, and they promised to serve the Lord.

After Joshua died, the Israelites ended up turning away from God. They did evil and worshipped other gods. Because of that, God stopped driving out the inhabitants of the land his people were to possess. When the Israelites went out to fight their enemies, God's hand was against them, and they were oppressed by their enemies. Eventually, the people cried out to God. It was at that time God began to raise up judges to deliver his people and lead them. While each judge lived, the people were faithful to God, but when the judge died, the people turned away from God. They would suffer at the hands of the land's inhabitants. And after a while, they would again cry out to God for help. Again, God would raise up a judge to help his people. That was a cycle that repeated itself again and again.

Eventually, the Israelites asked for a king like the other nations had. Even though God was their king, he let them have the kind of king they wanted. He appointed Saul to be the first king, and after awhile, Saul turned away from God. David, a young shepherd and a man after God's own heart, was chosen by God to become king after Saul. After David, his son Solomon was king. When Solomon died, his son became king. Israel rebelled, and the Israelite kingdom divided. Sadly, most of the kings who reigned in the two kingdoms were evil and did not follow God.

God still loved his people even when they turned their backs on him. He still wanted them to follow him with all their hearts, and he still wanted to bless them abundantly. He wanted them to live according to his commandments. No matter what evil his people had done or how many times they had been untrue to him, God continued to do things to bring them back to him.

And so God raised up prophet after prophet to tell his people he wanted them to return to him. The prophets told the people of the many blessings that could be theirs if they would return to God. The descriptions of those blessings were beautiful. How could the people not want to be obedient? But they weren't. The prophets also told the people how they would suffer at the hands of their enemies if they continued to disobey God. And yet, the people continued their disobedient lifestyle. God knew they would do that, and so he also told them the time would come when they would again be taken captive by other nations. They would be taken away to foreign lands.

The prophets also told them they would return from captivity. Again they would live in the land God had promised them. The prophets also told them of a deliverer, a Messiah, whom God would send to be their savior. He would save them from the consequences of sin.

Things happened just as God had said they would. They were taken captive, and eventually they returned to their own land.

Centuries passed, and God was still working out his plan to restore the relationship between himself and people—the relationship that had been spoiled by sin and death. The time was drawing near for that restoration to happen.

In the Bible, the Old Testament closes here, and the New Testament begins about four hundred years later. At the beginning of the New Testament, God sends the promised One, the Messiah, the Christ, the deliverer. He was called Jesus. He was God's own Son, and he was born to the virgin Mary. The Bible says, "the child grew and became strong; he was filled with wisdom, and the grace of God was upon him."[1] It also says, "Jesus grew in wisdom and stature, and in favor with God and men."[2]

Jesus lived life like other people did and experienced what other people experienced. He was tempted to sin and disobey God like all people are, but he never gave in to the temptation. He never sinned.

Jesus said the things God wanted him to say to his people. God still wanted his people to know him, and Jesus showed what God was like by the things he did and taught, as well as by how he related to people. Jesus said, "Anyone who has seen me has seen the Father."[3] Jesus wanted people to change the way they thought and lived. He taught about God's kingdom and how the relationship with God would be restored.

Jesus did much good on the earth. He showed people how to live a godly life, he healed the sick and blind, he fed the hungry and he was kind to those who were generally regarded with scorn. He had many faithful followers and yet, as with the prophets of old, men killed this One sent by God. Jesus was beaten, had nails hammered through his hands and feet and died a painful death hanging on a cross. Three days later, he rose from the dead. Not only did he come back to life, he also returned to heaven where he is seated at God's right hand. Jesus, the King of Kings, rules there in his kingdom. His subjects are those who follow him and are obedient to God. This was all part of God's plan, too.

After Jesus ascended to heaven, he sent his Holy Spirit to live in his followers and to remind them of what he had taught them. His followers began to preach and teach in the name of Jesus. This, too, was part of God's plan. His followers taught that Jesus is the Messiah, the Savior, and

[1] Luke 2:40
[2] Luke 2:52
[3] John 14:9

the only way to God. They told people that Jesus took the sins of the world with him to his death. God had said through the prophets that would happen. Jesus died to pay the debt for the sins of all people. People would not have to be punished for their own sins. Instead, Jesus was punished in our place. And because he died for our sins and rose to live again, those who obey him and who follow God with all their hearts can have their sins forgiven. Because Jesus died and then rose from the dead, people can again have a relationship with God. They do not have to be separated from God by sin and death.

Jesus' followers were baptized into Jesus, joining him in his death and resurrection, having their own sins forgiven, and receiving his Holy Spirit to live within each of them. His followers also taught how to live a life that was pleasing to God and told people about the many blessings they would experience while still on this earth.

Many people believed in Jesus and gave their lives to him as they obeyed God. They accepted that Jesus had come to save them from their sins and that through him, their relationship with God could be restored. Among those who believed and were saved were some who had participated in killing Jesus. God loved them and wanted to save them as much as he did anyone else. He wanted to bless them. In spite of the good news about Jesus, many people also rejected him.

As well as teaching those who didn't know Jesus, his followers also met together with other believers. Churches or gatherings of believers were found in many towns. The believers met together to worship God, to remember Jesus' death, burial, resurrection and ascension back into heaven and also to encourage one another to live faithfully and continually grow to be more like Jesus.

The Bible closes with a book that talks about the victory that is found in Jesus. It is a victory in which Satan, the tempter, is defeated. Sin and death were overcome. Jesus overcame them. That victory is one in which people can live forever with God. This, too, is God's plan.

God has promised a reward to those who are faithful to the end, even to the point of death. They will receive a crown of life. Those who have longed for Jesus' appearing will receive a crown of righteousness. Jesus said he would come back to take them to a place he has prepared for them. God has promised this home to those who love him to the end. There will be no death, no tears and no night there. It will be a holy city that will shine with the glory of God. God's followers will serve him there and see his face for eternity. God himself will be with his people forever and ever.

Throughout the Bible, God continually worked to carry out his plan to restore the relationship he had with man and woman before sin and death came between them. This was his plan even before the creation of the world. He carried this out through Jesus—through his life, death, burial, resurrection from the dead and his return to heaven. We can now have a relationship with God and Jesus, not only in this life, but also in the life to come. This is God's plan.

Questions for Thought

What did you learn about God from this chapter?

What kind of relationship does God want to have with people?

THE STORY OF A COVENANT GOD

Sometime after the beginning, God created the world in which we live. He appointed the sun to shine by day and the moon and stars to shine at night. The prophet Jeremiah said God made a covenant with the day and night to come at their appointed time[4].

God also made man. Actually, it was much more than that. God took some dust of the earth that he himself had made and from it he formed man. Then God breathed into man the breath of life, and man became a living being. But that wasn't all. God said, "Let us make man in our image, in our likeness."[5] That is what God did, and then he took a rib from the man, and from it, he made woman.

Adam and the woman, Eve, lived happily in the Garden of Eden for a while. They lived in obedience to God, but then Eve and Adam sinned. They ate from the one tree that was forbidden by God—the tree of knowledge of good and evil. God had promised death if they should eat from it, and God was true to his word. The man and woman's relationship with God changed when they disobeyed him. They experienced separation from God for the first time. Sin now stood between them and God.

It was at that time that God first said something about raising up someone who would defeat sin and death, who would defeat Satan. Meanwhile, Adam and Eve were banished from the garden. God had said there would be consequences for their disobedience, and there were. You see… God is always true to his word.

Time passed and the population on earth increased. With this increase, came another increase. Sin, the very thing that stood between people and God, was also increasing.

[4] Jeremiah 33:20
[5] Genesis 1:26

"The Lord saw how great man's wickedness on the earth had become, and that every inclination of the thoughts of his heart was only evil all the time. The Lord was grieved... and his heart was filled with pain."[6] God was grieved that he had made people, and he decided to wipe mankind from the face of the earth. He was going to bring floodwaters on the earth that would destroy everything on it.

At that time, there was a man named Noah. This one man found favor in the eyes of the Lord, and he walked with God. God had found Noah to be righteous.

God had a plan to save Noah, his wife, his three sons and his sons' wives from the floodwaters. He made a covenant with Noah. God told Noah what to do to be saved from the floodwaters. He told Noah how to build an ark and told him to fill it with certain animals. And do you know what? Noah did everything just as God commanded. And true to his word, God saved Noah and his family. When the floodwaters were gone, and Noah and his family came out of the ark, one of the first things he did was build an altar and sacrifice burnt offerings on it. "The Lord smelled the pleasing aroma and said in his heart: '...Never again will I destroy all living creatures as I have done...'"[7]

God said to Noah and his sons, "I now establish my covenant with you and your descendants after you and with every living creature... Never again will all life be cut off by the waters of a flood..."[8] God said that was an everlasting covenant, a covenant for all generations to come. The covenant was a promise God made to Noah, his descendents and all living creatures. To this day God has kept that promise.

[6] Genesis 6:5-6
[7] Genesis 8:21
[8] Genesis 9:9-11

God gave a sign of the covenant. The sign was a rainbow that he set in the clouds. God said that when he saw the rainbow, he would remember the covenant he had made with all life on earth.

Again the number of men on the earth increased and people were eventually scattered over the earth.

One day God spoke to a man named Abram. He told Abram to leave the land where he lived and go to a land God would show him. God said to him,

> "I will make you into a great nation and I will bless you; I will make your name great, and you will be a blessing. I will bless those who bless you, and whoever curses you I will curse; and all peoples on earth will be blessed through you."[9]

So, Abram left as God had told him to do. Near the town of Bethel he pitched his tent, built an altar to the Lord and called on the name of the Lord. Then he set out on his way again. As time passed and as Abram traveled about, he became a very wealthy man. Eventually, he came back to the place near Bethel. Scripture says that again Abram called on the name of the Lord there.

Later, the Lord's word came to Abram in a vision. God said to him, "Do not be afraid, Abram. I am your shield, your very great reward."[10]

God promised Abram a son from his own body to be his heir and promised him offspring as numerous as the stars in heaven. He promised to give land to Abram's descendants. Scripture tells us that on that day the Lord made a covenant with Abram to give his descendants the

[9] Genesis 12:2-3
[10] Genesis 15:1

land of Canaan.[11] The covenant was a sacred promise God made to Abram.

When Abram was 99 years old the Lord appeared to him to confirm his covenant. God changed his name to Abraham and his wife's name from Sarai to Sarah. He repeated the promises to Abraham concerning his offspring and that he would be the father of many nations. He said that kings would come from Abraham. God said that Sarah would be the mother of nations and that kings would come from her. He again said that he would give the land of Canaan to Abraham and his descendants. Then God said, "and I will be their God."[12] God gave a sign of his covenant with Abraham. The sign was circumcision—God's covenant in their flesh.[13] Abraham, his son Ishmael and the rest of the men in the household were circumcised that very day. The sign of circumcision was binding on Abraham, his male descendents and any males bought to become part of Abraham's household for generations to come. As part of the covenant, Abraham and his descendants were responsible for seeing that circumcision was carried out. God told Abraham that is what he had to do to keep God's covenant.

This covenant God made included sacred promises to Abraham concerning his offspring and a land of their own. It included a sign of the covenant—determined by God and carried out in the flesh by man. From this point forward, God's people would see his loyalty to this covenant as he acted in the interest of his people.

God also told Abraham that he would establish his covenant with Abraham's son, Isaac, whom Sarah would bear the next year.

---

[11] Genesis 15:18-21
[12] Genesis 17:8
[13] Genesis 17:9-14

Just as God had said, Isaac was born to Abraham and Sarah the next year. Isaac grew up and eventually married a woman named Rebekah. One night when Isaac was traveling, God appeared to him and renewed with him the covenant he had made with his father Abraham. He said,

> "I am the God of your father Abraham. Do not be afraid, for I am with you; I will bless you and increase the number of your descendants for the sake of my servant Abraham."[14]

Isaac built an altar there and called on the name of the Lord.

Isaac and Rebekah had two sons. It was to their son, Jacob, that God again renewed the covenant he had made with Abraham. God said to Jacob,

> "I am the Lord, the God of your father Abraham and the God of Isaac. I will give you and your descendants the land on which you are lying. Your descendants will be like the dust of the earth… All peoples on earth will be blessed through you and your offspring. I am with you and will watch over you wherever you go, and I will bring you back to this land. I will not leave you until I have done what I have promised you."[15]

The next morning, Jacob took a stone on which he had laid his head while sleeping, set it up as a pillar and poured oil over it. He also made an oath to God. God later changed Jacob's name to Israel, and God's people became known as the Israelites.

[14] Genesis 26:24
[15] Genesis 28:13-15

All this time God had been working to fulfill the promises of his covenant with Abraham. Sarah had born him a son, Isaac. Isaac had become Abraham's heir, just as God had said. Jacob, Abraham's grandson through Isaac, had 12 sons, and then their sons had sons. God was increasing the number of Abraham's descendants.

During a widespread famine, the Israelites fled to Egypt where there was food, and eventually they became enslaved to the Egyptians. God raised up Moses to deliver his people from slavery. He told Moses that he had appeared to Abraham, Isaac and Jacob and had established his covenant with them to give them the land of Canaan. It was because of his covenant with Abraham that God heard the Israelites in Egypt groaning about being slaves. God promised to free them from slavery and bring them to the land he had promised to Abraham, Isaac, and Jacob. God said, "I will take you as my own people, and I will be your God."[16]

After God led his people out of Egypt and they were camped near Mount Sinai, God told Moses to tell the people,

> "Now if you obey me fully and keep my covenant, then out of all the nations you will be my treasured possession. Although the whole earth is mine, you will be for me a kingdom of priests and a holy nation."[17]

God then gave Moses the Ten Commandments and the rest of the Law, telling him to "Write down these words, for in accordance with these words I have made a covenant with you and with Israel."[18]

[16] Exodus 6:7
[17] Exodus 19:5-6
[18] Exodus 34:27

If the Israelites kept the covenant with God, the blessings they experienced would be numerous. If they broke that covenant, the curses or disasters would also be numerous. God's people promised to fully obey him.

The Israelites then began their journey to the promised land, the land promised to Abraham, Isaac and Jacob and now to Moses and all of Israel. God told Moses he would drive out the people from the land they were to possess. God was fulfilling his promise to Abraham, the promise to give the land of Canaan to his descendants. As it turned out, it was not until about forty years later that the Israelites actually got to go into the promised land.

From the time God made his covenant with Moses and the Israelites until the time they finally entered Canaan, the promised land, the people griped and complained, they doubted God and his promises, and they broke the covenant with God. God punished their disobedience as he had said he would. And God is always true to his word. Still, he remembered his covenant with Abraham, Isaac and Jacob. According to his promise, he gave the Israelites the land of Canaan.

In the book Joshua it says,

> "So the Lord gave Israel all the land he had sworn to give their forefathers, and they took possession of it and settled there. The Lord gave them rest on every side, just as he had sworn to their forefathers. Not one of their enemies withstood them; the Lord handed all their enemies over to them. Not one of all the Lord's good promises to the house of Israel failed; every one was fulfilled."[19]

[19] Joshua 21:43-45

God was fulfilling his promise to Abraham—a promise that was already about six centuries old—a promise concerning the Land of Canaan. And according to his promise to Moses, God had given the people rest on every side.

The Israelites, in their disobedience to God, did not drive out all the people from the land. The worship of false gods, the sin and the wickedness remained. As time passed, the Israelites were influenced more and more by the people and their sinful ways.

Eventually, they asked for a king like the other nations had. God had already told the people through Moses that when they wanted a king, the king was not to accumulate wealth, wives, and powerful horses. God said he was to revere God, be humble and live according to God's word.[20] That was the kind of king God intended for them to have. Instead, they wanted one like the other nations. God said of them, "… they have rejected me as their king."[21] AND… God gave them the kind of king they wanted. He appointed Saul as their first king, but after awhile Saul turned away from God. God rejected Saul as king and had David anointed king. God said that David walked before him in "integrity of heart and uprightness,"[22] following God with all his heart.

As king, one of David's desires was to build a house for God—a place to put the sacred Ark of the Covenant[23] and a place for God to dwell. God denied David the privilege of doing that.

---

[20] Deuteronomy 17:14-20
[21] 1 Samuel 8:7
[22] 1 Kings 9:4
[23] The Ark of the Covenant was a chest-like piece of furniture that was kept in the Most Holy Place in the tabernacle or place of worship, and later in the temple. It is where God appeared and was so holy that no person was even supposed to touch it. Exodus 25:10-22; 2 Chronicles 5:7

He did make a covenant with David, though, in which he made many promises to him. He promised to make David's name great and said to David, "Your house and your kingdom will endure forever before me; your throne will be established forever."[24]

He promised to raise up a son to succeed David and to establish the throne of his kingdom forever. God told David that his son would be the one to do what David himself wanted to do, that is, to build a house for God. God said of David's son, "I will be his father, and he will be my son."[25] God said he would punish David's son when he did wrong. He also said, "But my love will never be taken away from him."[26]

David believed God's words. He knew how God had worked in the lives of his forefathers and that God had always been true to his word. David said,

> "How great you are, O Sovereign LORD! There is no one like you, and there is no God but you, as we have heard with our own ears. And who is like your people Israel—the one nation on earth that God went out to redeem as a people for himself, and to make a name for himself, and to perform great and awesome wonders by driving out nations and their gods from before your people, whom you redeemed from Egypt? You have established your people Israel as your very own forever, and you, O LORD, have become their God. And now, LORD God, keep forever the promise you have made concerning your servant and his house. Do as you promised, so that your name will be great forever. Then men

[24] 2 Samuel 7:16
[25] 2 Samuel 7:14
[26] 2 Samuel 7:15

will say, 'The LORD Almighty is God over Israel!'... O Sovereign LORD, you are God! Your words are trustworthy, and you have promised these good things to your servant."[27]

God had again shown himself to be true to his word. David's son, Solomon, was king after David. And just as God had told David, his son Solomon built the temple of God, the house David had wanted to build.

After Solomon's death, the kingdom of God's people divided into two nations, Judah and Israel. Many men served as kings over the two nations. God was fulfilling his promise to Abraham that kings would come from him and his wife, Sarah. He had promised that they would be the mother and father of many nations.

The kings over God's people were evil, for the most part. There were a few kings, though, who did what was right in the sight of God.

God's people, the Israelites, turned away from him many times. In order to communicate his will and his desire for his people to turn their hearts back to him, God raised up many prophets who told the people what God wanted them to know. He wanted them to know that if they continued in their sin and disobedience, punishment was certain to come. He knew their hearts, and therefore, he told them of captivity and exile that were to be part of their future. He told them of disaster and destruction they could not escape. And why was that going to happen? God, through the prophet Jeremiah, said it was because they had broken covenant with God. They had broken the covenant God had made with their forefathers.

[27] 2 Samuel 7:22-26,28

The prophets also brought hope for God's people. They spoke often of the One whom God would send to rescue his people. This One, the Messiah, would come from the seed of Abraham and of David. Jeremiah spoke of a new covenant that was yet to come. The prophets spoke of a covenant of peace, a covenant in which all of God's people would know him.

God was busy fulfilling the promise he had made when Eve and Adam sinned in the garden. He was busy fulfilling his covenant with Abraham, Isaac, Jacob, David and all of Israel.

True to his word, God did raise up One who would overcome sin and death. He would defeat Satan. He was of the seed of both Abraham and David. This One would rule in his kingdom forever. He was the promised Messiah, the Christ, Jesus, the Son of God, King of kings, Prince of Peace, the Root and Offspring of David. He was the hope of the prophets. He was and is the fulfillment of God's covenant with his people.

This Jesus, the Messiah, brought a new covenant—a covenant of peace, one based on better promises than the old one. In this covenant, God has put his laws in the minds and on the hearts of his people. His people are those who choose to follow him. They are those who give him their all. They are called the "children of Abraham."[28]

God invites us to join him in this covenant. When we do, we become "children of Abraham"[29]—children by faith in Jesus. God's promises are for us. He has redeemed us as a people for himself. He has chosen and made us, his people, to be a holy nation that he claims as his own. He has made us a kingdom of priests—a royal priesthood. He is our God.

[28] Galatians 3:7
[29] Galatians 3:7

Abraham looked forward "to the city with foundations, whose architect and builder is God."[30]   The writer of Hebrews says, "… you have come to Mount Zion, to the heavenly Jerusalem, the city of the living God. You have come to thousands upon thousands of angels in joyful assembly, to the church of the firstborn, whose names are written in heaven. You have come to God, the judge of all men, to the spirits of righteous men made perfect, to Jesus the mediator of a new covenant…"[31]

The New Testament closes with a book of VICTORY. It is a book of promise and hope. It looks to the future. John speaks of "the Holy City, the new Jerusalem, coming down out of heaven from God."[32] As he saw it, he also heard a voice saying, "Now the dwelling of God is with men, and he will live with them. They will be his people, and God himself will be with them and be their God."[33]

God chose us in Jesus "before the creation of the world to be holy and blameless in his sight. In love he predestined us to be adopted as his sons through Jesus Christ in accordance with his pleasure and will."[34] Even before the creation of the world, he had a plan to save people. Throughout the Bible, God was working to carry out his covenant.

God has given us a sign, a seal, and a deposit guaranteeing our inheritance until our redemption as God's possession. The sign of this covenant is the promised Holy Spirit of God whom he sends to live inside every person who believes in and follows Jesus.

Our God is a God of covenant! He is a God who is always true to his word, doing what he has promised.

[30] Hebrews 11:10
[31] Hebrews 12:22-24
[32] Revelation 21:2
[33] Revelation 21:3
[34] Ephesians 1:4-5

Questions for Thought

As you think about God's actions down through the ages, how do they illustrate his faithfulness to the covenant he made with Abraham?

How have you seen God being true to his word in your life?

A CHOSEN AND HOLY PEOPLE

"In the beginning God created the heavens and the earth."[35]

On the sixth day of creation, God created out of the ground all the animals and birds. Then, on that day, God also did something he had never done before. He created a being in his own image and likeness. He took some dust of the earth that he had made, and from it he formed man. He breathed into man the breath of life, and man became a living being—a being created in the image and likeness of his Creator. That day when God, the Creator, looked at all he had made, he considered it very good.

God said it wasn't good for man to be alone. He had no suitable helper. So, from the man who was made in God's own image and likeness, God took a rib and from it he made a suitable helper for man. The man called her woman. They were Adam and Eve.

Adam and Eve lived in a garden in Eden. God had put trees in the garden that were pleasing to the eye and good for food. He provided plenty of water for the garden. He also provided for and took care of the man and woman. He assigned the man to take care of the garden and work it.

Once, as God walked in the garden in the cool of the day, he called to the man. The man did something he had never done before. He answered God but told him he was afraid and had hidden when he heard his Creator walking in the garden. You see, the woman and the man had done the one thing their Creator and God had told them not to do. They had eaten from the tree of knowledge of good and evil.

[35] Genesis 1:1

They had become more like the Creator in that they knew not only good, but also evil. And things changed between them and their Creator. Death had entered the world. Sin and disobedience now stood between them and God. The Creator, God, said there would be consequences for Eve and Adam's sin. One consequence was that they were banished from the Garden of Eden and would no longer walk and talk there with their Creator.

There were also other consequences, one of which involved pain. Adam would experience it as he worked the earth for food and Eve as she gave birth to children.

Their Creator, God, offered one ray of hope. The serpent who had tempted Eve was cursed. The Creator said that One would someday crush the serpent's head and defeat him. Sin and death would be overcome eventually.

After being banished from the garden, Eve gave birth to sons. Time passed, and their sons had wives and families. The number of people on the earth continued to increase.

Sin also increased and was rampant on the earth. The wickedness was so great that God grieved that he had made people, and his heart filled with pain. He decided that he would wipe mankind, the animals and the birds from the face of the earth by sending a flood to destroy all life.

But there was one man on the earth who found favor with God—a man who lived in fellowship with God. God decided to save this man, Noah, and his family. Noah obediently built an ark and filled it with animals exactly as his God had told him to do. Noah and his family went into the ark, and God closed the door.

The flood came and destroyed life outside the ark. Noah and his family were saved by God, though. When they came out of the ark, Noah sacrificed burnt offerings to

God, and the aroma of the sacrifices pleased God. He promised to never again destroy all life by a flood, and he put a rainbow in the sky to remind himself of his promise.

People again multiplied and covered the earth. Many, many years passed, when one day, God spoke to a man named Abram. He told Abram to leave his country, his people and his father's household. God said he would show Abram where to go and would bless Abram. Abram left his home and went where God led him. Sometimes he found it hard to trust God, but God was always with him. He never left him and was always true to his word.

God said he would make Abram into a great nation through whom all the people on earth would be blessed. He promised to give Abram's descendants a land of their own and said that kings would come from him and his wife. These promises were part of the covenant God chose to make with Abram. The covenant was a special agreement between God and Abram's family. It involved promises, a sign and a special relationship. God was Abram's provider, his reward and his shield.

God changed Abram's name to Abraham and his wife Sarai's name to Sarah. He also promised that within a year, Abraham's wife, who was past childbearing age, would bear him a son who would be named Isaac. And just as God had said, he began to bless Abraham. Within a year, Sarah gave birth to Isaac. God had finally given Abraham an heir through his wife, Sarah. Circumcision was given as a sign of the covenant, and all male members in Abraham's household had to be circumcised. Abraham made sure circumcision was done to all the males in order to keep the covenant with God.

Isaac grew up and married Rebekah. He became the father of two sons, Jacob and Esau. It was through Jacob that God intended to fulfill his covenant promises to Abraham. God told Jacob that his descendants would be like the dust of the earth, that all people on earth would be blessed through him and his offspring and that God would bring Jacob back to the land that God had promised to Abraham's descendants. God changed Jacob's name to Israel and his descendants, God's chosen people, became known as the Israelites.

Jacob became the father of twelve sons. His favorite son was named Joseph. Joseph's brothers hated him because his father loved him more than he loved any of them. Their hatred grew, and when the opportunity presented itself, Joseph's brothers sold him into slavery. Then they convinced their father that his beloved son, Joseph, was dead.

Joseph ended up being a slave in Egypt. Still, God continually cared for Joseph, and Joseph prospered even as a slave. The Lord gave him success in all he did, and he found favor in people's eyes again and again. The Egyptian, Potiphar, who was the captain of the guard, and then Pharaoh, the ruler of Egypt, each gave Joseph a great deal of authority and power. God revealed to Joseph that there would be a time of plenty in the land followed by a time of famine. It was then that Pharaoh put Joseph in charge of the land of Egypt, second-in-command only to himself, so Egypt would survive the famine when it came.

God blessed Joseph in Egypt by giving him two sons, Manasseh and Ephraim. Joseph said God had made him forget all his troubles and had made him fruitful in the land of his suffering.

It was during the famine that Joseph again saw his brothers. Not knowing Joseph was there, they went to Egypt to buy grain for themselves and their families. Joseph's brothers were terrified when they realized they were talking with their brother. Joseph told them not to be troubled. He said it was not them, but God who had sent him to Egypt. It was part of God's plan. Joseph recognized that his brothers had intended to harm him. He also recognized and later told his brothers that God had intended it for good to save many lives. Joseph was in Egypt for a reason. God had chosen him to play a vital role in the survival of the Israelites during the famine. As a result of their meeting, Joseph's father, brothers and their families all moved to Egypt where Joseph could provide for them during the remainder of the famine.

Jacob died while he was in Egypt, and as God had told him, his dearly loved son, Joseph, was with him at his death. Eventually, Joseph also died in Egypt, as did his brothers and all that generation of people. The Israelites were fruitful, and there were so many of them that the land was eventually filled with Israelites. A new Pharaoh ruled over Egypt. He didn't know about Joseph and what he had done for Egypt. Because the Israelites were so numerous, he decided to make them slaves. After a while, the people finally cried out because of their slavery, and God heard them.

God planned to rescue his people from slavery using a man named Moses. Earlier, God had saved Moses from death when the new Pharaoh, trying to reduce the number of Israelites in the land, had all their baby boys killed. God was now ready to use Moses to free his people.

The job God had for Moses was not an easy one. First, he had to convince the elders of the Israelites that God had actually given him the job of leading them out of Egypt and slavery. Then he had to convince Pharaoh to let God's people go. But God had chosen him, and he was not on his own. God worked through Moses to inflict plagues on Egypt, and finally Pharaoh was convinced to let God's people go free.

Just as God had planned, Moses led the Israelites out of Egypt and out of slavery. Once they were out of Egypt and God had led them as far as Mount Sinai, he had some special things to say to these people he had chosen as his own. Speaking through Moses he said to them,

> "You yourselves have seen what I did to Egypt, and how I carried you on eagles' wings and brought you to myself. Now if you obey me fully and keep my covenant, then out of all nations you will be my treasured possession. Although the whole earth is mine, you will be for me a kingdom of priests and a holy nation."[36]

Moses later told the people, "For you are a people holy to the Lord your God. The Lord your God has chosen you out of all the peoples on the face of the earth to be his people, his treasured possession."[37] Moses told them the reason why God had chosen them. He said, "It was because the Lord loved you and kept the oath he swore to your forefathers."[38] He said it was not because they were so numerous, but because they were the least of all the nations.

God led his servant Moses up Mount Sinai. There he spoke to Moses giving him the Ten Commandments and all his law for his people. This law would govern God's people for over a thousand years.

After giving his law to the Israelites, God continued leading his people toward Canaan, the land he had promised to give them. When God's people arrived there, some men went to explore the land. Of those who went in to explore, only two, Joshua and Caleb, believed and trusted God. The others didn't believe God would really do what he had said. They didn't believe he would fight for them and would drive the people out of the land before them. Instead, they became afraid and didn't trust God. God forgave the

[36] Exodus 19:4-6
[37] Deuteronomy 7:6
[38] Deuteronomy 7:8

people but said none of them would enter the promised land except for Joshua and Caleb. God said only the people's children would get to see the promised land and that he would bring them into the land to enjoy it.

As a result of their sin and distrust, the Israelites wandered in the desert for forty years. At the end of that time, all the generation of those who had not trusted God when they were first brought to the promised land had died. Of that generation, only Moses, Joshua and Caleb still lived. Moses had sinned in the desert, and God did not allow him to enter the promised land either. Moses climbed Mount Nebo, and from there God showed him the promised land. Then Moses died and was buried.

God chose Joshua to be the new leader of his people. He promised to be with Joshua just as he had been with Moses. He also cautioned Joshua to be strong and courageous and to obey all his law. If he did that, God said, Joshua would be prosperous and successful in all he did. He also said he would be with Joshua wherever he went.

Joshua led the people into the promised land, and God began to drive out its inhabitants before the Israelites. Joshua allocated the land to each tribe as God had commanded. Time passed, and God gave the Israelites rest from all their enemies. After that, Joshua called together all the tribes of Israel and reminded them of what God had done for them. He told them to "fear the Lord and serve him with all faithfulness... But if serving the Lord seems undesirable to you, then choose for yourselves this day whom you will serve... But as for me and my household, we will serve the Lord."[39] The people said they, too, would serve the Lord.

[39] Joshua 24:14-15

Joshua sent the people away to take possession of the land each tribe had been given by the Lord. Joshua then died and was buried in the land that was his inheritance. After that, the generation of people died who knew what God had done for the Israelites. Another generation grew up, and they turned away from the Lord and served other gods. Consequently, the Lord's hand was against them, and he delivered them into the hands of their enemies. As a result, the people suffered greatly. They were oppressed by their enemies, and their land was devastated.

Eventually, the people cried out to God for help, and he raised up judges to lead his people and to deliver them. The Bible says,

> "Whenever the LORD raised up a judge for them, he was with the judge and saved them out of the hands of their enemies as long as the judge lived; for the LORD had compassion on them as they groaned under those who oppressed and afflicted them. But when the judge died, the people returned to ways even more corrupt than those of their fathers, following other gods and serving and worshiping them. They refused to give up their evil practices and stubborn ways."[40]

God said he would no longer drive out before them the nations who were still left in the land God had promised to give his people. Therefore, they suffered greatly at the hands of their enemies. Each time the oppression would become so great that they would cry out to God for help and deliverance. And each time, God, in his compassion, would raise up a judge who would deliver the Israelites and be their leader. Some of the people God chose to lead and judge Israel were Deborah, Gideon, and Samson.

[40] Judges 2:18-19

It was during the time of the judges that God heard the prayer of a woman named Hannah. Hannah had no children, and while she was worshiping at Shiloh, she prayed fervently, asking God for a son. She told God that if he would give her a son, she would give him to God all the days of his life. God heard her and granted her request. She named her son Samuel, and she kept her word to God. When Samuel was still a small child, Hannah took him to the priest at Shiloh. Each year when she and her husband went to make their annual sacrifice there, Hannah took a robe to her son. There at Shiloh, Samuel served the Lord. God was with him as he grew, and he chose Samuel to be the final judge for Israel. He appeared to Samuel at Shiloh and also chose him to be his prophet. Scripture says, "The Lord continued to appear at Shiloh, and there he revealed himself to Samuel through his word. And Samuel's word came to all Israel."[41]

When he grew old, Samuel appointed his sons to serve as judges for Israel. His sons did not live lives that honored God. Because of that, Israel decided they wanted a king like the other nations, rather than having judges to rule over them.

God knew they would someday ask for an earthly king. When God had given the law to Moses, Moses told the people what God said about the kind of king they would need. He said that the king they appoint must be chosen by God. He was not supposed to accumulate horses, wives, or wealth. Nothing was to turn the king's heart away from God. In fact, he was to write for himself a copy of God's law and was to read it daily. That would help him learn to honor God through obedience and to live and serve humbly as king.

[41] 1 Samuel 3:21-4:1

Then, when the people asked for the kind of king the other nations had, God listened to them. While having a king would make them like the other nations, it would also have its disadvantages. God told Samuel to warn the people what it would be like to live under a king. And so Samuel told the people that they would be servants of the king and that he would take their sons and daughters and make them his own servants. He would also take their slaves, and the best of their fields, olive groves, vineyards and livestock. He said to the people, "When that day comes, you will cry out for relief from the king you have chosen, and the LORD will not answer you in that day."[42] The people refused to listen to the warning and still wanted a king who would lead them and take them into battle.

God knew the people were rejecting him as their king and, yet, God granted their request. He gave them the kind of king they wanted.

It was Samuel who anointed the first king. God chose an impressive young man named Saul to be king. After a while, God was sorry that he had made Saul king because Saul had become disobedient to him. Therefore, God "sought out a man after his own heart"[43] that he could appoint as the king and leader of his people. The young man God chose was a shepherd named David. God told David, "You will shepherd my people in Israel, and you will become their ruler."[44] David was a man after God's own heart, a man who enjoyed God's favor. His relationship with and dependence on God is seen in the many psalms David wrote.

David lived a long life. Before he died, he made his son, Solomon, king in his place. God had told David that he would be with Solomon and would discipline Solomon when needed, but he would never take his love away from

[42] 1 Samuel 8:18
[43] 1 Samuel 13:14
[44] 2 Samuel 5:2

him. "God gave Solomon wisdom and very great insight, and a breadth of understanding as measureless as the sand on the seashore... He was wiser than any other man."[45] It was Solomon who was chosen by God to build the first temple in Jerusalem.

When Solomon died, his son Rehoboam became king. Israel rebelled against Rehoboam, and the nation of Israel became a divided kingdom. The northern kingdom, Israel, was first ruled by a king named Jeroboam, and the southern kingdom, Judah, was ruled by Solomon's son, Rehoboam. Each kingdom had a long succession of kings. Some of the kings followed the ways of the Lord, but most did not. Israel and Judah fought against each other, as well as against other nations. War became a commonplace thing for the Israelites.

God had told his people again and again that if they obeyed his laws and followed him with all their heart, he would bless them richly. He had also told them that if they worshipped other gods and did not obey the Lord God, there would be unpleasant consequences. And God's love for the nation of Israel never changed. He still loved them and wanted them to obey and follow him with all their heart. He wanted to shower on them the abundant blessings that would come with their obedience.

God raised up prophet after prophet to call his people back to him. God gave the prophets the words he wanted them to speak to his people. He said to the prophet Jeremiah, "Before I formed you in the womb I knew you; before you were born I set you apart; I appointed you as a prophet to the nations...You must go to everyone I send you to and say whatever I command you. Do not be afraid of them, for I am with you and will rescue you..."[46] The prophets told the people that if they would return to God, he would receive them back and bless them bountifully. If they would

[45] 1 Kings 4:29, 31
[46] Jeremiah 1:5,7-8

not return, the curses or disasters they would experience would be manifold. God knew the hearts of the people. He knew they were not going to turn back to him, so he also told them of the disasters they would have to suffer. He said a time of captivity was a definite part of their future.

The prophets did not have an easy or pleasant task. The people were, for the most part, not receptive to the messages from God. Elijah, one prophet chosen by God, said, "I have been very zealous for the LORD God Almighty. The Israelites have rejected your covenant, broken down your altars, and put your prophets to death with the sword. I am the only one left, and now they are trying to kill me too."[47]

The prophets also brought hope for God's people. God wanted them to know that they would return to the land he had promised to them and that he would raise up a Messiah or Savior. This Messiah would be called the Holy One of God. He would be God's chosen one, one in whom he delights. And yet God would willingly allow him to suffer for his people. The prophet Isaiah said that the Messiah would be despised by men and rejected by them, he would be familiar with suffering, he would be pierced for our sin and rebellion and he would be led to slaughter like a lamb. The Holy One of God would bear the sins of many. And finally, the Messiah would triumph. He would crush the head of Satan and would defeat sin and death.

At that time, the disobedient Israelites continued to suffer at the hands of their enemies. They were eventually taken into captivity. The northern kingdom was the first to be taken captive. Then the southern kingdom, with Jerusalem, was taken captive. Many of God's people were exiled and lived in a land that was not their own just as they had done centuries before in Egypt.

---

[47] 1 Kings 19:10

Time passed, and, as God had promised, some of the Israelites returned to their war-torn homeland. They saw the destruction that had taken place in Jerusalem. With their return from exile, the temple in Jerusalem was finally rebuilt, and eventually, the wall around Jerusalem was also reconstructed.

God continued to send prophets to his people while the exiles were still returning to Jerusalem. The prophets confronted the people about their sin, and they still spoke of the coming Messiah. God still admonished his people to set their heart on honoring him. He still wanted them to revere him and stand in awe of his name. He wanted them to follow his ways. He told his people he wanted to "throw open the floodgates of heaven and pour out so much blessing that you will not have room enough for it."[48] And yet the people still did not return to God.

The Bible is silent about what happened during the 400 years between the end of the Old Testament and the beginning of the New Testament.

Then one day, an angel appeared to a young virgin named Mary. He told her she had found favor with God, that the Holy Spirit would come upon her and that she would be with child. He said the Holy One to whom she would give birth would be called the Son of God.

And it happened just as the angel said. The baby was born and was named Jesus. Just as he had promised, God had sent his chosen One, the promised Messiah, his own Son. Jesus grew up in the home of Mary and her husband, Joseph. Jesus "grew and became strong; he was filled with wisdom, and the grace of God was upon him."[49]

When he was about 30 years old, Jesus began to teach about the kingdom of God. He called people back to a way

[48] Malachi 3:10
[49] Luke 2:40

of living that was pleasing to God. He also did many miracles—healing the sick, the lame, and the blind. He fed the hungry and cast out evil spirits. Many people were amazed when they saw and heard Jesus. Some people, especially the religious leaders, were angry and wanted to kill him. Jesus challenged what they taught and what they practiced. He wanted them to truly live according to God's word.

Jesus had many followers during the years he went about teaching and doing miracles. His followers were called disciples. One night, as Jesus often did, he went out alone to pray. Then he called his disciples to him, and from them, he chose twelve men to be apostles. These men worked closely with Jesus and spent much time with him. From these twelve, Jesus had three to whom he was especially close. They were Peter, James and John. There were times when Jesus wanted to be with just these three.

Jesus knew what God's plan was concerning his time here on earth. Because his time was short, he wanted to prepare the apostles for what was going to happen. Jesus told them that he must suffer many things and be rejected by Israel's leaders. He said he would be handed over to the Gentiles (people who were neither Israelites nor Jews) who would mock him, insult him, flog him and kill him. Then, on the third day, he would rise from the dead. Jesus also said he would not leave his followers alone. He said he would send the Comforter, the Spirit of Truth, to be with them. He said the Spirit would teach them and remind them of what Jesus had said to them. And he said the Spirit would testify about him. Jesus told his disciples that they, too, must testify about him because they had been with him from the beginning.[50]

Jesus was arrested, rejected, mocked and beaten, and, just as God had planned, Jesus was finally hung on a

---

[50] John 15:27

cross to die. On that cross he carried on himself our sins. The sins of the entire world were on Jesus, the Holy One of God. He was the Messiah, the Deliverer, and the Savior to which God's people had looked forward.

Jesus was taken from the cross, buried and, on the third day after that, he rose from the dead. This Jesus, the Son of Man, the Savior of the world was and is alive. He had overcome sin and death and had crushed the head of Satan.

And then, it was time for Jesus' disciples to go to work. Jesus had opened the way for restoring the relationship between people and God. He had provided for all people's sins to be forgiven. Jesus wanted the whole world to know about that and so he told his disciples, "…go and make disciples of all nations, baptizing them in the name of the Father and of the Son and of the Holy Spirit, and teaching them to obey everything I have commanded you. And surely, I am with you always, to the very end of the age."[51]

In the sight of his followers, Jesus was taken up into heaven. Then his followers began spreading the gospel, the good news about Jesus. Many believed their message and committed their lives to Jesus. As with the prophets and with Jesus, however, many did not believe, and they rejected God's words. They rejected Jesus. They rejected God himself. And they persecuted Jesus' followers. His followers were arrested, beaten, flogged, imprisoned, stoned, and killed. And in the face of all that, they remained true to God, never denying him. They followed him with all their heart, obeyed his word and served him with all faithfulness. And, as God had always done, he blessed them for their obedience.

God sent his own Holy Spirit to live inside each of his people. And he continues to do that today. God blesses his

[51] Matthew 28:19-20

people with a peace that passes all understanding. When we are tempted to sin, like Eve and Adam were, God provides us a way of escape. He also forgives our sin.

God makes his people into a new creation. He transforms us by giving us a new spirit and heart—a heart of flesh instead of a heart of stone—and by renewing our minds.[52] As God's people, we "put on a new self, created to be like God in true righteousness and holiness."[53] We reflect God's glory as we are transformed into his likeness. God's followers are a new creation—created to be like their God and Creator. It is he who makes us new.

The people who follow Christ are referred to as the body of Christ.[54] We make up the church, a body in which every part, every person fills an important role. And if one part of the body suffers, it affects the whole body. That is because God intends for his people to live and serve in community, as one. They did it in the Old Testament, they did it in the New Testament and we do it now.

Jesus' followers wrote and taught much about this community. They told the people to encourage each other and build each other up. They were told to motivate each other to do good works and to love each other. Meeting together was important for encouraging one another, for worship and for taking part in the Lord's Supper.[55] They were to confess their sins to each other and pray for each other. Christ's followers, Christians, faced opposition, persecution and trials. Therefore, prayer, encouraging each other, and having the support of community were of utmost importance. Scripture says, "Therefore as God's chosen people, holy and dearly loved, clothe yourselves with compassion, kindness, humility, gentleness and patience. Bear with each other and forgive whatever

[52] Ezekiel 36:24-27; Romans 12:2
[53] Ephesians 4:24
[54] 1 Corinthians 12:27
[55] 1 Corinthians 11:20-34

grievances you may have against one another... Let the peace of Christ rule in your hearts, since as members of one body you were called to peace. And be thankful."[56]

God chose us in Jesus before the creation of the world. His plan was to send Jesus to save people from the sin that would stand between them and their God. Sin no longer has to come between people and God. According to his plan, God has provided a way for people and God, their Creator, to be together in eternity.

We will walk and talk with our God. As a matter of fact, we will spend eternity in the presence of our God and Creator. The Bible says that even Abraham who lived so long ago looked forward to a city whose builder is God. He looked forward to a heavenly home. One of the last things recorded in God's word to his people concerns that home. About it, scripture says, "Now the dwelling of God is with men, and he will live with them. They will be his people, and God himself will be with them and be their God."[57] It also says, "He will wipe every tear from their eyes. There will be no more death or mourning or crying or pain, for the old order of things has passed away."[58] The glory of God will give it light, and Jesus will be its lamp. There will be no night, and the city gates will never be shut. It is in that place that God's chosen people will spend eternity. We will live forever in the presence of our God and Creator.

As God said to his people so long ago, he says to those today who wholeheartedly commit their lives to him, "you are a chosen people...a holy nation, a people belonging to God."[59] That is what we are—a chosen and holy people.

---

[56] Colossians 3:12-13, 15
[57] Revelation 21:3
[58] Revelation 21:4
[59] 1 Peter 2:9

Questions for Thought

What was the plan God had from before the creation of the world? How does that affect your belief in him?

How might really believing that you were chosen by God and belong to him affect the way you live your life from day to day?

THE PROMISED ONE

From the time Adam and Eve sinned in the Garden of Eden, God had promised the coming of One who would crush the tempter's head.

God promised Abraham that all nations would be blessed through him and his seed.[60] He renewed that promise with Abraham's son, Isaac, and later with Jacob, Abraham's grandson.[61]

Moses told the people that God would raise up a prophet like him from among the Israelites and that they should listen to this One.

God made a promise to King David that he would establish his house and throne forever. That was to be accomplished through the One whom God had been promising to send. David spoke often in the Psalms about the promised One. He said this One would be hated without reason, and he described what it would be like for him as he would suffer death. He said that the hands and feet of this One would be pierced.[62] People would stare and gloat over him. His garments would be divided, and people would cast lots for his clothing. David said that not one of his bones would be broken and that God would not abandon this One to the grave or let him see decay.

Through the prophet Isaiah, God said a virgin would be with child and would give birth to a son who would be called Immanuel, which means God with us. He would grow up and preach good news to those who were poor and freedom to those who were captives. He would "proclaim the year of the Lord's favor..."[63] He would also be

[60] Genesis 12:3
[61] Genesis 26:2-4; 28:13-14
[62] Psalm 22:16
[63] Isaiah 61:2

rejected and despised by men. He would be familiar with suffering and would carry our sufferings and sorrows. Isaiah said, "But he was pierced for our transgressions, he was crushed for our iniquities; the punishment that brought us peace was upon him, and by his wounds we are healed … the LORD has laid on him the iniquity of us all. He was oppressed and afflicted, yet he did not open his mouth; he was led like a lamb to the slaughter."[64] This One would be numbered with sinners and rebels. Isaiah said that after that happens, "he will see the light of life and be satisfied."[65] He would justify many and would intercede for sinners.

God revealed through the prophet Micah that it would be from the town of Bethlehem that he would bring forth One to rule Israel.

Jeremiah prophesied concerning the slaughter of babies to be born about the time of the One whom God would send.

God revealed through Zechariah that this One, a king, would come riding on a donkey. He also revealed that the inhabitants of Jerusalem would look on this One whom they would pierce and that they would mourn for him. God also told Zechariah that this One, a shepherd, would be struck and the sheep would be scattered.

God sent prophet after prophet to try to turn his disobedient people back to him. The prophets reminded the people again and again how much God wanted their obedience and wanted them to love him with all their hearts. The prophets told them how God wanted to bless them so abundantly. They also told the disobedient people what the consequences of their disobedience would be and how they would suffer because of turning their backs on God.

[64] Isaiah 53:5-7
[65] Isaiah 53:11

Thankfully, the prophets also brought God's message of hope as they told the people of this One whom God would send to deliver and redeem them. It was through this One that Israel's deliverance was to come.

The Old Testament closes with the words spoken by God through the prophet Malachi. God said that the Lord the people are seeking will come and he will be the messenger of the covenant.

After that, we don't hear from God for about 400 years. And then... about two thousand years after the promise to Abraham and a thousand years after the promise to David... IT WAS TIME.

An angel from God appeared to a young woman named Mary. She was a virgin and was pledged to marry a man named Joseph. The angel told her she had found favor with God and would give birth to a son whom she would name Jesus. Mary didn't understand how that could be true since she was a virgin. The angel explained to her, "The Holy Spirit will come upon you, and the power of the Most High will overshadow you. So the holy one to be born will be called the Son of God... For nothing is impossible with God."[66] Jesus would be the Son of God. He would be "Immanuel—which means 'God with us.'"[67]

An angel also appeared to Joseph, the man who was betrothed to Mary, and told him the child to be conceived in Mary would be from the Holy Spirit. He also told Joseph not to be afraid to take Mary as his wife, and so he did take her to be his wife.

Then one night, in the town of Bethlehem, the baby Jesus was born. An angel appeared to some shepherds nearby as they were watching their sheep and told them that they brought news that would result in great joy. A Savior had

[66] Luke 1:35, 37
[67] Matthew 1:23

been born, and he was Christ the Lord. Then a host of angels appeared to them, praising God. When the angels left, the shepherds went into Bethlehem to see the baby. Then they spread the news about what had happened and what they had heard from the angels. They glorified and praised God.

According to the law, Joseph and Mary took Jesus to Jerusalem to present him to the Lord. When they went into the temple courts, there was a righteous and devout man there who held Jesus in his arms and proclaimed him to be God's salvation and light to the Gentiles and the Israelites, that is, to all people. A prophetess was also there at the temple. Coming up to them, she thanked God and told about the child Jesus to those who were looking for Jerusalem to be redeemed.

Some wise men came to Jerusalem asking about the One who had been born king of the Jews. They said they had seen his star and wanted to worship him. When King Herod heard about it, he was very disturbed. He called together those who knew the law and asked where this One, the Christ, was supposed to be born. They told him what had been said through the prophet Micah: this One, Jesus, was to be born in Bethlehem. Herod wanted the wise men to go to Bethlehem to find the baby and then report back to him. The wise men left there and traveled on, following the star, until it led them to Jesus. They worshipped him, giving him expensive gifts, and then, instead of reporting back to Herod, they returned home.

Meanwhile, King Herod searched for the young Jesus in order to kill him. He even gave orders to kill all baby boys living in and around Bethlehem who were two years old and younger. Jesus was safe, though, for an angel had appeared to Joseph in a dream and warned him to flee with his family to Egypt. Then, when Herod died, Joseph was told to take his family back to Israel. He did, and they settled in the town of Nazareth in the district of Galilee.

Scripture says, "And the child grew and became strong; he was filled with wisdom, and the grace of God was upon him."[68] When Jesus was twelve years old, he went with his family to Jerusalem for the annual Passover Feast. He went to the temple courts and talked with the teachers there. He listened and asked questions. All who listened to him were amazed at how much he understood and at the answers he gave.

Jesus had a cousin named John the Baptist who, like the prophets, had also been sent by God. He was to prepare the way for God's promised One, Jesus. People wondered if John might be the One God had promised—the Messiah. He told people that there was one coming after him who was more powerful than he. John also preached a baptism of repentance for the forgiveness of people's sins.[69]

When Jesus was grown, he went to John to be baptized. "As Jesus was coming up out of the water, he saw heaven being torn open and the Spirit descending on him like a dove. A voice came from heaven: 'You are my Son, whom I love; with you I am well pleased.'"[70] Testifying to what had happened, John said Jesus was the Son of God. He also called Jesus the Lamb of God who would take away the sins of the world.

After Jesus' baptism, the Spirit led him into the desert where he spent forty days and forty nights fasting. Satan tempted him there, and Jesus relied on God's word to fight Satan. After tempting Jesus repeatedly, the devil finally left him "until an opportune time,"[71] and God's angels attended to Jesus.

---

[68] Luke 2:40
[69] Mark 1:4, Luke 3:3
[70] Mark 1:10-11
[71] Luke 4:13

Jesus then began to teach the people about God—how to live for him, how to love him, and what his kingdom was like. News about him spread. In his hometown, Jesus was rejected. Going into the synagogue on the Sabbath, he read from the prophet Isaiah, "The Spirit of the Lord is on me, because he has anointed me to preach good news to the poor. He has sent me to proclaim freedom for the prisoners and recovery of sight for the blind, to release the oppressed, to proclaim the year of the Lord's favor."[72] Jesus told the people he was the fulfillment of that prophecy. At first, they were amazed. As he continued to speak, they became furious and drove him out of town.

Jesus called men to follow him. He told people that if they would come to him, he would give them the bread of life, and they would never go hungry. He said he would give them living water, and he promised people rest for their souls. He said he would raise up his followers in the last day and that they would have eternal life. Jesus gathered quite a following as he traveled and taught the people.

Once, after spending the night in prayer, Jesus called together his disciples, those who followed him. From among them, he picked twelve men and appointed them to be apostles. Those twelve men spent the rest of Jesus' life traveling and working closely with him. He taught them what they needed to know so they, too, could do the Father's work.

Jesus continued to travel about the country teaching about the kingdom of God. He described it again and again, using different word pictures. He wanted the people to understand what his Father's kingdom was really like.

When Jesus saw crowds of people, he had compassion on them. He healed their sick, their lame, and their blind. He cast out evil spirits. He rid people of many diseases and

[72] Luke 4:18-19

illnesses. Two blind men once called out to Jesus when they heard he was going by. The people told them to be quiet, but they only called out louder. Jesus heard them and had compassion on them. He touched their eyes and healed them immediately. Another time, when a man with leprosy came to Jesus, Jesus was filled with compassion and healed him. The more people Jesus healed, the more the news about him spread. People were overwhelmed, amazed, astonished, and filled with awe at what they saw Jesus do. They praised God because of what he was doing.

People followed Jesus long distances—sometimes even until they ran out of food. The Bible tells about two different times when Jesus fed the hungry who were with him. Because of his compassion, he did not want to send them away hungry. His disciples couldn't imagine how they could feed as many people as were with them. Once, there were five thousand men, not including women and children. The other time the men numbered four thousand. Jesus knew his power and what he could do. We only know that he gave thanks for the little bit of food they did have and then had the disciples distribute it to the people. They all ate until they were satisfied, and each time, there was much food left over.

Jesus spent a great deal of time teaching the people. He wanted them to understand more fully what God's will was. Men had distorted God's laws and commandments, and Jesus explained to the people what God had really meant and what he wanted from the people. He called for people to live differently. He wanted them to turn away from the way they had treated God's laws and begin to really live in obedience—willingly and gladly from their hearts.

Some people were amazed at the authority with which Jesus taught. The religious leaders, on the other hand, were often challenged by what Jesus said. They had decided for themselves what the laws meant, and Jesus' teaching was often in disagreement with what the religious leaders taught. Therefore, they were often angry with Jesus.

Jesus also had the power to raise people from the dead. Once, seeing a funeral procession and knowing the dead person was the only son of a woman who was a widow, Jesus' heart went out to the woman. He raised her son from the dead. The people were in awe of Jesus and praised God. Another time, Jesus raised a friend of his from the dead. Jesus was actually called while the man was sick but decided to wait before going to him. Jesus said this happened "for God's glory so that God's Son may be glorified through it."[73] Arriving at his friend's home, Jesus was deeply moved when he saw his friend's sister crying because her brother had died. Jesus also cried. He was again deeply moved as he came to the tomb where his friend had been buried. He had the stone rolled away from the tomb, and after praying, he called for his friend to come out. His friend did as Jesus wanted and came walking out of the tomb alive. Because of this miracle, many people believed in Jesus. Some people told the religious leaders what had happened, and the leaders became so disturbed about it that they began to plot against Jesus, looking for a way to take his life. They even planned to kill Jesus' friend because when people heard how Jesus had raised him from the dead, they began to follow Jesus and believe in him.

The religious leaders had been looking for a way to arrest Jesus for some time. With them making plans now to kill Jesus, he needed to begin preparing his disciples for what was soon to happen. He told them he would suffer, be rejected and be betrayed. He was going to be condemned to die and would be killed. He said that on the third day, though, he would rise from the dead.

[73] John 11:4

51

Soon after that, the Bible says, "Having loved his own who were in the world, he now showed them the full extent of his love."[74] Wrapping a towel around himself, Jesus filled a basin with water and began to wash and dry the feet of those apostles who were with him—those to whom he was closest. He told them he had set an example that they should follow. He had already told them that whoever wanted to be great must be a servant and must serve just as Jesus had come to serve. He, their Lord and Teacher, had washed their feet as an example for them and as a true expression of his love for them.

When it was time for the annual celebration of the Passover, Jesus told his apostles he had eagerly desired to eat the Passover meal with them before he would suffer. As he ate with them, he took the bread and said it was his body, which would be given for them. He took the cup and said it was his blood, the blood of the new covenant, which would be poured out for many. He told them to eat and drink it in memory of him.

He told his disciples he was going back to his Father's house to prepare a place for them and would come back for them. He explained to the disciples how he and the Father are one. He said that anyone who had seen him had really seen the Father. Everything Jesus said was what the Father wanted him to say. The Father lived in Jesus and worked in and through him. In fact, they were and are one.

Jesus also told them he would not leave them alone. He said he would send God's Spirit to be with them forever. The Spirit would comfort them, teach them and remind them of everything Jesus had said to them. The Spirit would also testify about Jesus, and he would convict the world of guilt in regard to three things—sin, righteousness and judgment.[75]

[74] John 13:1
[75] John 16:8-11

Jesus had come from the Father and was now returning to him. He told his disciples they would grieve for a while, but then their grief would be turned to joy. Jesus wanted his joy to be in them, and he wanted that joy to be complete. He told them that when they saw him again, they would rejoice with a joy that no one could take from them.

Jesus also wanted to prepare his apostles for how they would respond to the things that were about to happen to him. The prophet Zechariah had said Jesus' followers would be scattered, and he wanted to prepare them for and reassure them concerning that. He said, "But a time is coming, and has come, when you will be scattered, each to his own home. You will leave me all alone. Yet I am not alone, for my Father is with me. I have told you these things, so that in me you may have peace. In this world you will have trouble. But take heart! I have overcome the world."[76]

Taking with him the three apostles to whom he was closest, Jesus went, as he often did, to spend time with his Father in prayer. Jesus said to the apostles, "My soul is overwhelmed with sorrow to the point of death. Stay here and keep watch with me."[77] Jesus prayed, "My Father, if it is possible, may this cup be taken from me. Yet not as I will, but as you will."[78] Praying a second time, he said, "My Father, if it is not possible for this cup to be taken away unless I drink it, may your will be done."[79] A third time, he prayed the same prayer. While Jesus prayed, those he had asked to keep watch with him had fallen asleep.

Jesus knew his time had arrived. In prayer he said, "Father, the time has come. Glorify your Son, that your Son may glorify you... I have brought you glory on earth by

[76] John 16:32-33
[77] Matthew 26:38
[78] Matthew 26:39
[79] Matthew 26:42

completing the work you gave me to do. And now, Father, glorify me in your presence with the glory I had with you before the world began."[80] And he asked the Father to protect his followers from the evil one.

Then Jesus was betrayed by one of the twelve who had worked so closely with him. Jesus knew that would happen and so was not surprised when the man arrived with soldiers and some of the religious leaders to arrest Jesus. One of the apostles struck a servant of the high priest with his sword, cutting off his ear. Jesus touched the man's ear and healed him. And he told his disciple to put his sword away. Jesus said he had angels at his disposal, but that things must happen this way. Jesus would drink the cup his Father had given him. He would do his Father's will.

Only a few days earlier, Jesus had ridden into Jerusalem on a donkey. People had spread their cloaks and branches on the ground as Jesus rode along, and they had shouted, "Blessed is the king who comes in the name of the Lord!"[81] and "Blessed is the coming kingdom of our father David!"[82] and "Hosanna to the son of David!"[83]

In sharp contrast to that, Jesus was now betrayed and arrested. Going before various officials, he was questioned, and many gave false testimony about him. He was stripped, dressed in a crown made of thorns and a purple robe, and then made a mockery of. The soldiers cried out, "Hail, king of the Jews!"[84] Jesus was ridiculed, spit on, slapped, blindfolded and beaten. He was condemned to die.

Jesus' disciples scattered and left him alone. At least one was there, though, seeing what was happening to Jesus.

[80] John 17:1, 4-5
[81] Luke 19:38
[82] Mark 11:10
[83] Matthew 21:9
[84] John 19:3

One of those closest to Jesus was asked three times if he was Jesus' disciple or if he knew Jesus. And three times he denied knowing him. Jesus had told him that would happen. He had said he would deny him three times before the rooster crowed. As soon as he denied Jesus the third time, the rooster did crow, and Jesus looked straight at the man. Remembering what Jesus had said to him, he went out and wept bitterly.

As the ruler stood with Jesus before the people, the crowd yelled, "Crucify him! Crucify him!"[85] The ruler had Jesus flogged and then handed him over to the people to do what they wanted with him. And so… a cross was placed on the already beaten and bleeding back of Jesus, and he began the trip to Golgotha, a place right outside of the city of Jerusalem. On the way, the cross was taken from him and put on the back of another man. The trip continued. People followed Jesus, wailing and mourning for him.

Upon reaching Golgotha, nails were driven through Jesus' feet and hands and into the cross. And there on the cross, Jesus hung, suffering the pain of having been beaten, having carried his own cross partway to Golgotha, having nails hammered into his hands and feet and having to bear the weight of his body on those nails. He also carried on him the tremendous weight of the sins of all people who had or who ever would live. Before he died, while hanging on the cross, this Savior, so full of love, cried out concerning the people to whom he had been handed over, "Father, forgive them, for they do not know what they are doing."[86] Afterwards, Jesus said, "Father, into your hands I commit my spirit."[87] He cried aloud, and then he died.

JESUS WAS DEAD. The promised One was dead. The Son of God, the Lamb of God who would take away the sins of the world had been killed.

[85] Luke 23:21
[86] Luke 23:34
[87] Luke 23:46

Later, soldiers came and broke the legs of the two criminals who had been crucified with Jesus. They didn't break Jesus' legs, because he was already dead. Just like King David had said so long ago, not one of his bones was to be broken. Instead, they pierced his side with a spear, and blood and water poured out of his body.

Two of Jesus' disciples asked to have his body. They took the body down from the cross, wrapped it with spices in linen strips, and put it in a tomb that was nearby.[88] And Jesus' followers mourned and wept.

Then, on the third day, some of Jesus' followers went to the tomb. The stone had been rolled away. Going into the tomb, they saw that Jesus' body was no longer there. It was gone. Angels appeared and spoke to some women who had gone to the tomb and told them JESUS HAD RISEN and that they would see him in Galilee. They reminded them of what Jesus himself had told them on several occasions. He had said he would be killed, and on the third day he would rise from the dead. The women were afraid, yet they were also filled with joy.

JESUS WAS ALIVE! He had overcome death! He had defeated Satan! JESUS, THE CHRIST, THE PROMISED ONE, LIVED AGAIN!!!

After he rose from the dead, Jesus appeared to and talked to many of his followers. He appeared to women, to the twelve, to his disciples and even to more than five hundred people at one time. Jesus told his followers that what had happened was just as he had said it would be. He said all the prophecies about him must be fulfilled. He opened their minds so they could understand the scriptures. He reminded them that the Spirit, the Counselor and Comforter, would be sent by the Father to them. And he

---

[88] John 19:38-42

told them to make disciples, baptizing them and teaching them to obey all Jesus' commands. Jesus promised to be with them. He told them to stay in Jerusalem until they received power when the Holy Spirit would come on them. Then, lifting his hands, Jesus blessed them and was taken up into heaven. There he sat down at the right hand of God.

Jesus' disciples were told then that he would come back in the same way they had seen him go up into heaven.

His disciples did what Jesus had told them to do. They waited in Jerusalem until the Spirit came on them with power. And just as Jesus wanted, they spent their lives teaching the good news about Jesus and making disciples.

They taught that God took Jesus, who had no sin, and made him to be sin for us, for all people.[89] Jesus died in our place, for our sins. Through Jesus' death and burial, God reconciled the world to himself. Through Jesus' resurrection and ascension back into heaven, he gave us the hope of living eternally in God's presence. When we make Jesus the Lord of our lives, when we join him in his death, burial and resurrection,[90] we begin a new life. We are made new. We begin to live for Jesus, the Savior, the Messiah, the Promised One.

That is not the end of the story, though. Jesus said he would come back to take his followers home to a place he has prepared for them. Before his death, Jesus had prayed, "Father, I want those you have given me to be with me where I am, and to see my glory, the glory you have given me because you loved me before the creation of the world."[91]

[89] 2 Corinthians 5:21
[90] Romans 6:3-11
[91] John 17:24

JESUS, THE SON OF GOD, THE PROMISED ONE, IS COMING BACK!!!! Jesus said that those who follow him will be raised up in the last day and will have eternal life. Jesus is coming back to take his followers home to be with him forever!

From the time of Adam and Eve, God had spoken of the Promised One. Moses talked of this One. David spoke of him many times in the Psalms. Prophet after prophet repeated the message from God of the coming of the Promised One. This One was the Savior God had promised to his people. He was the One who carried the sins of the world to his death. He crushed the head of the tempter, Satan. He was the One who overcame sin and death and now offers hope to God's people, to everyone who would follow Jesus, the Promised One.

Questions for Thought

What was there about Jesus that would make people look forward to his coming?

Considering the things that happened in Jesus' lifetime, why do you think he submitted to God's plan for his time on earth?

THE LAW LEADS TO CHRIST

*"So the law was put in charge to lead us to
Christ that we might be justified by faith.
Now that faith has come, we are no longer
under the supervision of the law."*
Galatians 3:24, 25

The Bible begins with the account of God creating the heavens with the sun, moon, and stars and the world with all the plant and animal life. God created Adam and Eve and placed them in the Garden of Eden. There they walked and talked with God. After a while, they disobeyed God. Because of their decision to disobey, sin and death came between them and God. And God put Adam and Eve out of the garden. Outside the garden, they worked the earth and had children.

Time passed and the number of people on earth increased. Wickedness and evil also increased, and God, in grief and with pain filling his heart, decided to destroy all life on earth with a flood. A man named Noah found favor with God, and God decided to save him and his family. He told Noah to build a large boat called an ark into which he, his family and some of the animals were to go. When they were in the ark, God sent the flood and destroyed all life outside the ark. Only eight people were saved from the flood. When the waters had receded, the eight people in Noah's family and the animals came out of the ark.

The number of people increased and became scattered throughout the land. One day God spoke to a man named Abram. He told Abram to leave his home and his people and go to a land that God would show him. God made a covenant with Abram in which he promised to bless Abram and his descendants. He said he would give them a land of their own. He even said he would bless all people through Abram. Abram obeyed God and went where God led him.

God changed Abram's name to Abraham and blessed him and his wife, Sarah, with a son in their old age. Their son's name was Isaac. He grew up, married and had twin sons named Jacob and Esau. Jacob, whose name God changed to Israel, had twelve sons. His sons and their descendants became known as the Israelites.

One of Jacob's sons, Joseph, was sold into slavery by his brothers who hated him. Afterwards, they were able to convince their father that his beloved son, Joseph, was dead.

Joseph ended up as a slave in Egypt where he found favor with people again and again. One of the people with whom he found favor was the Pharaoh, or king of Egypt. Pharaoh had two dreams which none of his wise men could interpret. But God revealed those dreams to Joseph and enabled him to interpret the dreams. Joseph said there were to be seven years of plenty in the land followed by seven years of famine. Pharaoh decided there was no one as wise as Joseph, so he put Joseph in charge to prepare the country of Egypt for the famine. The famine came, and many people were without food. Jacob and his family were among those who were without. They had heard that there was grain in Egypt, and so Jacob's sons went there to buy some. They were taken to Joseph and asked if they could buy grain. They didn't recognize Joseph, though. On their second trip to Egypt, Joseph finally revealed himself as their brother and asked them to move their families there, so he could see that they were provided for during the remainder of the famine.

And so it ended up that Jacob and his entire family lived in Egypt. Things went well for them for a long time. Eventually, there was a Pharaoh who didn't know about Joseph. Because the Israelites had become so numerous, the Pharaoh decided to enslave them. The Egyptians made life very bitter for the Israelites, and they finally cried out to God. God heard them and sent his servant, Moses, to rescue them. Pharaoh was stubborn, and God ended up sending many plagues on Egypt before Pharaoh finally told Moses that he would let God's people go. The Israelites set out for the Red Sea where God parted the waters so they could cross on dry land. The Egyptians pursued them, and when they got to the Red Sea and tried to cross behind the Israelites, God closed the waters, and the Egyptians drowned.

From there God led his people, the Israelites, to Mount Sinai where they camped for awhile. It was there that God gave his people the Ten Commandments and the rest of his law. The law included rules for keeping peace and for dealing with sin. It included rules concerning sexual matters, injuries and diseases. Protection of people's property and the treatment of servants were included in God's law. It emphasized justice, mercy and doing good. It also included much about how they were to worship God.

God gave Moses very detailed instructions for building the Tabernacle.[92] The Tabernacle was to be the center of the Israelites' worship of God. God said it would be a sanctuary for him and that he would dwell among his people. The people were to carry it with them as they traveled, and each time they stopped to camp, they would set up the Tabernacle.

The Tabernacle or Tent of Meeting was a rectangular tent-like building surrounded by a rectangular courtyard enclosed in a series of posts and crossbars from which hung curtains. It was a beautiful place with curtains of blue, purple and scarlet. There was much gold, silver and bronze in it.

When entering the courtyard, the first thing a person came to was an altar for burnt offerings. It was on this altar that animal sacrifices were made to God. Next, there was a

[92] Exodus 25:1-28:43; 30:1-6, 17-21

basin in which the priests washed before making a burnt offering or before entering the Tabernacle. When the priests entered the Tabernacle, they were in a rectangular room called the Holy Place. In it were a candlestick made of pure gold, an altar of incense that was overlaid with gold and a gold covered table on which was placed the bread of the Presence.[93]

Behind the Holy Place was the Most Holy Place. There was a curtain dividing the two areas. In the Most Holy Place was the Ark of the Covenant. It was a chest overlaid inside and out with pure gold. The cover was also made of pure gold and had two cherubim on it with their wings spread upward and facing each other. Poles were put through gold rings on each corner to carry it. Among other things, the tablets of stone given to Moses by God on Mount Sinai were put inside the Ark of the Covenant.[94]

Only the priests could go into the Holy Place in the Tabernacle, and only once a year could the high priest enter the Most Holy Place.

Once the tabernacle was finished and was erected according to God's instructions, God's glory filled it.

God also gave very specific instructions about the priests' clothing.[95] He described in detail what the high priest's garments were to be like. He was to wear a tunic of fine linen and a robe made of blue cloth with blue, purple and scarlet around the hem. The robe had gold bells around the hem. He wore a piece called an ephod. It was made of linen and gold with blue, purple and scarlet yarn. On it were two onyx stones on which were engraved the names of the twelve sons of Israel, six on each stone. The high

---

[93] The significance of this bread is not stated explicitly in the Bible, but it may represent God's presence in the Tabernacle and his presence with man as his provider.
[94] Exodus 25:16; Deuteronomy10:1-5
[95] Exodus 28:1-43; 39:1-31

priest also wore a breastplate for making decisions. It was made of gold, of blue, purple and scarlet yarn and of linen. There were twelve precious stones on it, one for each of the twelve tribes of Israel. The name of each tribe was engraved on a stone. The Urim and the Thummim were placed in it so they would be over the heart of the high priest. The turban had a plate or diadem of pure gold attached to it on which was engraved "Holy to the Lord".[96] The high priest also wore a sash.

The other priests were to have tunics, sashes and headbands "to give them dignity and honor".[97] After being dressed in their special clothing, the men had to be consecrated so they could serve God as priests. Moses' brother, Aaron, and Aaron's sons from the tribe of Levi were chosen by God to be the priests. Aaron was appointed as the first high priest. God told Moses what to do to anoint and ordain them as priests to serve God. The Levites,[98] of the tribe of Levi, were also set apart by God to help the priests with the duties at the Tabernacle.

God gave specific instructions about what was to be done each day at the Tabernacle. Certain animal and grain sacrifices were to be made each day. God said to Moses,

> "For the generations to come this burnt offering is to be made regularly at the entrance to the Tent of Meeting before the LORD. There I will meet you and speak to you; there also I will meet with the Israelites, and the place will be consecrated by my glory. So I will consecrate the Tent of Meeting and the altar and will consecrate Aaron and his sons to serve me as priests. Then I will dwell among the Israelites and be their God. They will know that I am the

[96] Exodus 28:36
[97] Exodus 28:40
[98] Exodus 32:26, 29

LORD their God, who brought them out of Egypt so that I might dwell among them. I am the LORD their God."[99]

God also gave details about what was to be offered as a sacrifice, why it was to be offered and when it was to be offered. There were burnt offerings, grain offerings and fellowship offerings. There were daily, weekly and monthly offerings. God said the offerings were a pleasing aroma to him.

He told the people that even if they sinned unintentionally,[100] they were still guilty and would be held responsible. And so he provided for them to make a sin offering so they could be forgiven. The sin sacrifice involved slaughtering an animal that was without defect. Depending on the situation, the animal might be a bull, a goat, a lamb, doves or pigeons. If a person could not afford even two pigeons or doves, he could bring a specified amount of flour.

Only once each year, on the Day of Atonement,[101] could the high priest enter the Most Holy Place. There, in a cloud over the atonement cover is where God appeared to the high priest. The high priest was to bring burning coals and incense into the Most Holy Place. The smoke from the incense would hide the atonement cover so that the high priest would not die. He was to bring with him to the entrance of the Tabernacle two goats. He was to choose one as a sin offering and the other as a scapegoat.[102] He was to kill the sin offering and take its blood with him into the Most Holy Place. On that day, the high priest would make atonement for himself, the people, the Most Holy Place, the Tabernacle and the altar. After he had done all that, he was to take the scapegoat, put on its head all the

[99] Exodus 29:42-46
[100] Leviticus 4:13-35
[101] Leviticus 16:2-34
[102] Leviticus 16:20-22

sins of Israel and then send it out into the desert where it was released. Concerning the Day of Atonement, God said to the Israelites,

> "This is to be a lasting ordinance for you: On the tenth day of the seventh month you must deny yourselves and not do any work—whether native-born or an alien living among you—because on this day atonement will be made for you, to cleanse you. Then, before the LORD, you will be clean from all your sins. It is a sabbath of rest, and you must deny yourselves; it is a lasting ordinance. The priest who is anointed and ordained to succeed his father as high priest is to make atonement. He is to put on the sacred linen garments and make atonement for the Most Holy Place, for the Tent of Meeting and the altar, and for the priests and all the people of the community. This is to be a lasting ordinance for you: Atonement is to be made once a year for all the sins of the Israelites."[103]

In addition to observing the Day of Atonement, God commanded his people to keep various feasts.[104] They were to keep the Sabbath weekly as a day of rest. They were also to observe a Sabbath Year. God commanded the people to observe annually the Feast of Weeks, the Feast of Trumpets and the Feast of Tabernacles. God appointed a Year of Jubilee.[105] Another feast the people were to observe was the Passover, which included the Feast of Unleavened Bread.

The Passover was a time set aside to remember when God had brought his people out of Egypt. The last plague

---

[103] Leviticus 16:29-34
[104] Leviticus 23:1-44; 25:1-55
[105] Leviticus 25:8-55

God had sent on Egypt was the death of every firstborn son and every firstborn of all the livestock in the land. When they were in Egypt, the Israelites were told to kill a lamb or goat and put its blood on their doorframes. God had told them the blood would be a sign for them, and when he saw the blood, he would pass over them and not permit the destroyer to kill their firstborn. And that night around midnight, in every place that did not have blood on the doorframe, every firstborn son died. There was much mourning and wailing in Egypt that night, and the Israelites were able to leave Egypt then.

God told them to observe the Passover and the Feast of Unleavened Bread annually. It was to be done only in the place God chose as a dwelling for his name. They were to slaughter the Passover lamb and sacrifice it in the evening, when the sun was going down. The lamb was to be a year old and without defect. None of its bones were to be broken. The meat was to be roasted and eaten according to God's word, with bitter herbs and bread that had no yeast in it. For seven days they were not to possess or eat yeast.

These commandments were intended to govern and guide God's people for generations to come. Moses wrote down the commandments and later told the priests to read the law to the people every seven years.[106] Moses also told the people that, in addition to obeying God's laws, God also wanted them to love him with their whole being. The law was important and so was their love and devotion to God.

After the law was given to Moses and the Israelites and after the Tabernacle was completed, God led his people toward the land he had promised to give them—the land promised to Abraham, Isaac, Jacob and all their descendants. When they got to the promised land, the

---

[106] Deuteronomy 31:9-13

people did not trust God. As a result, they did not get to enter the land to take possession of it at that time. Instead, they wandered in the wilderness for about forty years. Moses was their leader all during the wilderness wanderings but died before the Israelites finally entered the promised land. Joshua became the leader that took them into the land God had first promised to Abraham for his descendants.

The people began taking possession of the land as God drove out its inhabitants. After Joshua led the people in taking possession of it, he died. It wasn't long until the people began to follow other gods and worship them. They were influenced by other nations and by the people they had not driven out of the lands God had given them.

Eventually, the Israelites asked for a king like the other nations had. God's desire was for their king to be one who would live humbly, obediently and faithfully before God, trusting in him.[107] The people wanted a king who would lead them and take them into battle. They wanted to be like the other nations.

God gave them the kind of king they wanted. Saul was the first king but eventually he turned away from God and no longer obeyed him. God rejected him as king and chose David, a man after God's own heart, to be king. After David, his son, Solomon was chosen to be king. Solomon built the first Temple[108] for God's Name in the city of Jerusalem. The basic layout of the Temple was like that of the Tabernacle; they both contained the Holy Place and the Most Holy Place. When the Temple was finished, King Solomon had the Tabernacle and the Ark of the Covenant brought to the Temple. The priests took the Ark of the Covenant into the inner sanctuary or Most Holy Place. Afterwards, the people sang and praised God. "Then the temple of the LORD was filled with a cloud, and the priests

[107] Deuteronomy 17:14-20
[108] 2 Chronicles 3:1-2, 5:1, 6:7-10

could not perform their service because of the cloud, for the glory of the LORD filled the temple of God."[109] God told his people, "Now I have chosen Jerusalem for my Name to be there."[110]

After Solomon died, the Israelite kingdom divided. It became two nations—Israel to the north and Judah to the south. Jerusalem, the place God had chosen for his name to be, was in Judah. Many kings ruled over Israel and Judah. Most of the kings were evil and did not follow God. The people tended to follow the king whether he was faithful or unfaithful to God. When the Israelites didn't follow God, he raised up prophets time after time to warn them to turn from their evil ways and return to him. The people most often chose to not listen, and God, who was slow to anger,[111] became very angry[112] with them.

They were attacked again and again by the nations surrounding them, and eventually, because they had sinned against God, they were taken captive. The Assyrians took Israel captive, and then Judah was taken captive by the Babylonians. The Israelites were exiled to foreign lands, lands not their own.

Eventually, many of the Israelites came back to live in the land God had promised them. They worked on rebuilding the Temple, which had been destroyed. They also rebuilt the wall around Jerusalem. Soon after the rebuilding, the Old Testament ends.

The New Testament begins about four hundred years after the Old Testament closes. It begins with the birth of Jesus, the Son of God. He was called the Holy One of God. He was called the Son of Man and Rabbi or Teacher. He was the promised Messiah or Christ. John the Baptist said

[109] 2 Chronicles 5:13-14
[110] 2 Chronicles 6:6
[111] Exodus 34:6-7; Nehemiah 9:17; Jonah 4:2
[112] Jeremiah 25:1-7, 44:2-8

about Jesus, "Look, the Lamb of God, who takes away the sin of the world!"[113]

When Jesus was grown, he went about teaching and doing miracles. He challenged people's behavior and their thinking about God's laws and what God wanted from them. He was compassionate and healed many, many people. He showed people grace and mercy. He met people's needs and taught them about God and his kingdom. He showed what God is like by his words, his actions and how he related to people. Jesus did much good in the short time he lived on this earth. He also gathered quite a following, including some who were very close to him.

People's reactions to Jesus varied tremendously. Some people were amazed and astonished at him and what he did. Others became angry with him and wanted to kill Jesus.

Jesus knew it was God's will that he would die for the people. He knew when the time drew near that he would have to return to Jerusalem and face those who wanted to kill him.

When the time was finally near and it was the Passover, Jesus met with his disciples in Jerusalem to celebrate it and the Feast of Unleavened Bread. While doing so, Jesus took the unleavened bread and told his disciples, "Take and eat; this is my body."[114] Taking the cup, the fruit of the vine, he said, "Drink from it, all of you. This is my blood of the covenant, which is poured out for many for the forgiveness of sins."[115]

Jesus asked the Father to take this cup of death from him if possible. If it wasn't possible, though, and if Jesus had to

[113] John 1:29
[114] Matthew 26:26
[115] Matthew 26:27-28

die, he would. He wanted to do God's will. And he would do it voluntarily, freely giving up his life for the life of all people.

Jesus was arrested and beaten. With nails hammered through his hands and feet, he hung on a cross to die. He was led like a sheep to the slaughter and shed his blood. Those who were crucified at the same time as Jesus had their legs broken so they would die more quickly. Jesus was already dead when the soldiers came, and they did not break his legs. Instead, they pierced his side with a spear. On the cross, like Jesus had said, his blood was "poured out for many for the forgiveness of sins."[116] He carried our sins with him to his death. Jesus gave his life for the people of this world.

And when he died, the curtain in the earthly Temple was torn in two from the top to the bottom. The blood of Jesus had opened the way into the Most Holy Place.[117]

Jesus was buried and then rose from the dead. After his resurrection from the dead, Jesus entered heaven, the true sanctuary or Most Holy Place. Unlike the high priests under the old law, Jesus did not enter the Most Holy Place by the blood of goats and calves. Instead, he entered by his own blood—the blood of the covenant, shed for many for the forgiveness of sins. In shedding his blood, Jesus was a sin sacrifice that was spotless, without sin or defect. He was the Son of Man and the Son of God. And unlike the sin sacrifices made by the high priests, Jesus was a sacrifice that only had to be offered one time. Scripture tells us,

> "For Christ did not enter a man-made sanctuary that was only a copy of the true one; he entered heaven itself, now to appear for us in God's presence. Nor did

[116] Matthew 26:28
[117] Hebrews 9:12

he enter heaven to offer himself again and
again, the way the high priest enters the
Most Holy Place every year with blood that
is not his own. Then Christ would have had
to suffer many times since the creation of
the world. But now he has appeared once
for all at the end of the ages to do away with
sin by the sacrifice of himself... so Christ
was sacrificed once to take away the sins of
many people..."[118]

God had prepared a body for Jesus[119], a body of flesh and
blood, and it was that body that was the perfect sacrifice
for the sins of the world. The debt for our sins was paid
"with the precious blood of Christ, a lamb without blemish
or defect."[120] Jesus, the Lamb of God, obtained eternal
redemption by his blood. The cleansing was not an
outward cleansing like under the old law. It was an inward
cleansing—a cleansing of the conscience.[121]

Not only was Jesus our sin sacrifice, he also became our
high priest. The high priest under the old law had to enter
the Most Holy Place once every year to make atonement
for his own sins and the sins of the people. When the high
priest died, someone else replaced him. God himself
appointed Jesus to be high priest forever and says about
him,

"... because Jesus lives forever, he has a
permanent priesthood. Therefore he is able
to save completely those who come to God
through him, because he always lives to
intercede for them. Such a high priest meets
our need—one who is holy, blameless,
pure, set apart from sinners, exalted above

[118] Hebrews 9:24-26, 28
[119] Hebrews 10:5
[120] 1 Peter 1:19
[121] Hebrews 9:14

the heavens. Unlike the other high priests, he does not need to offer sacrifices day after day, first for his own sins, and then for the sins of the people. He sacrificed for their sins once for all when he offered himself."[122]

Jesus, our high priest, lived on earth as a man and so, experienced what we do. He was tempted in every way, even though he did not sin. Because of that, he understands our weaknesses. He appears for us in God's very presence, and he intercedes for us. Scripture says, "Therefore, brothers, since we have confidence to enter the Most Holy Place by the blood of Jesus, by a new and living way opened for us through the curtain, that is, his body, and since we have a great priest over the house of God, let us draw near to God with a sincere heart in full assurance of faith..."[123] When Jesus died and the curtain was torn, he opened the way for us to enter the Most Holy Place—to be in the very presence of God.

The Most Holy Place that Jesus, our high priest, entered was the true one. "When Christ came as high priest of the good things that are already here, he went through the greater and more perfect tabernacle that is not man-made, that is to say, not a part of this creation."[124] The earthly Tabernacle was man-made. Moses made it according to the pattern he was shown on Mount Sinai. That sanctuary was "a copy and shadow of what is in heaven."[125] Jesus entered the true sanctuary, heaven itself, and is in God's presence there, seated at his right hand.

According to God's command, it was from the tribe of Levi that the priests came. Jesus was not of the tribe of Levi. Instead, he was personally appointed by God to be high

[122] Hebrews 7:24-27
[123] Hebrews 10:19-22
[124] Hebrews 9:11
[125] Hebrews 8:5

priest[126]. With this change in the priesthood, there also had to be a change in the law. The new law would make men perfect or complete. Scripture says, "By one sacrifice he has made perfect forever those who are being made holy."[127]

The ministry Jesus has received as our high priest is superior to the old priesthood. That is because Jesus is the mediator of the new covenant that is founded on better promises. God promises, with the new covenant, to write his laws on our hearts and put them in our minds. We will know him. He will forgive us and not remember our sins.[128]

Jesus is our sin sacrifice and our great high priest. Through shedding his blood as our sacrifice, Jesus, who is also our high priest, has opened the way into the true sanctuary, the true Most Holy Place. He has entered that sanctuary, heaven, and is in God's presence interceding for us.

Jesus is also our Passover lamb.[129] In Jerusalem when, according to the law, the people were killing their Passover lambs, Jesus, the Lamb of God, was also being killed. He was dying on a cross as our Passover lamb. And, as it was in Egypt, the blood that was shed provides protection from death. For us, though, the protection is from eternal death.

Paul, one of Jesus' apostles, wrote that when we are baptized, we die and are buried with Christ. He said,

> "... just as Christ was raised from the dead through the glory of the Father, we too may live a new life. If we have been united with him like this in his death, we will certainly also be united with him in his resurrection.

[126] Hebrews 5:4-6
[127] Hebrews 10:14
[128] Hebrews 8:6-12
[129] 1 Corinthians 5:7

> For we know that our old self was crucified with him so that the body of sin might be done away with, that we should no longer be slaves to sin... Now if we died with Christ, we believe that we will also live with him. For we know that since Christ was raised from the dead, he cannot die again; death no longer has mastery over him. The death he died, he died to sin once for all; but the life he lives, he lives to God."[130]

And so we, having been made alive to God, are not to let sin reign in our bodies.

At Passover, the Israelites were to get rid of the leavening in their houses. We are to do the same thing. We are to get rid of wickedness and malice and are to celebrate "with bread without yeast, the bread of sincerity and truth."[131] Jesus is not only our Passover Lamb, he is also the truth[132] and the bread of life.[133] In him, we celebrate, now and forever, the life God gives us.

Jesus, our sin sacrifice, our high priest and our Passover lamb, will return to this earth, but not to die again and not to offer himself as a sacrifice again. Instead, he will come to bring salvation and eternal life.

I can't help but wonder if God's attention to all the details concerning the law, the feasts, the Tabernacle, the priesthood and the sacrificial worship was because of the magnitude and beauty of who Christ is and what he has done for us. Perhaps, too, it is because of all that is involved in living in a relationship with God.

[130] Romans 6:4-6, 8-10
[131] 1 Corinthians 5:8
[132] John 14:6
[133] John 6:35, 48

When God gave Moses the pattern for the Tabernacle, he said it would be a sanctuary for him, and he would dwell among his people. Remember that the Tabernacle, with its worship and sacrifices, was "a copy and shadow of what is in heaven."[134]

The New Testament closes with John talking about the New Jerusalem that was coming down out of heaven. About it he says, "Now the dwelling of God is with men, and he will live with them. They will be his people, and God himself will be with them and be their God."[135] He also says there is no temple there "because the Lord God Almighty and the Lamb are its temple."[136]

After he was raised from the dead, Jesus said, "Everything must be fulfilled that is written about me in the Law of Moses, the Prophets and the Psalms."[137] Scripture says that the law of Moses "is only a shadow of the good things that are coming—not the realities themselves."[138] "So the law was put in charge to lead us to Christ..."[139] Jesus Christ is the fulfillment of the law. He is our sin sacrifice, our high priest, our Passover Lamb and so much more.

The realities are found in Christ. The realities include, among other things, forgiveness of our sins, being reconciled to our God and living joyfully by his power and in his presence forever. It includes living and serving in relationship with other believers and enjoying the blessings associated with these realities.

> "As you come to him, the living Stone— rejected by men but chosen by God and precious to him—you also, like living stones,

[134] Hebrews 8:5
[135] Revelation 21:3
[136] Revelation 21:22
[137] Luke 24:44
[138] Hebrews 10:1
[139] Galatians 3:24

are being built into a spiritual house to be a holy priesthood, offering spiritual sacrifices acceptable to God through Jesus Christ... But you are a chosen people, a royal priesthood, a holy nation, a people belonging to God, that you may declare the praises of him who called you out of darkness into his wonderful light."[140]

These are the good things God has for us. The law has truly led us to Christ. And, in Christ, we have come to God.

Questions for Thought

How did the law lead us to Christ?

What does Christ offer that is better than what the law offered?

[140] 1 Peter 2:4-5,9

THE GOD OF COMPASSION AND HOPE

God created the heavens and the earth. On the first day, he separated light from the darkness and made day and night. On the second and third days, he made the sky, the seas, and plant life. On the fourth day, he made the sun, moon and stars. Then, on the fifth and sixth days, he made all living creatures.

When God created man and woman, they had a special relationship with God. The man and woman, Adam and Eve, lived in the Garden of Eden where God provided for all their needs. God even walked about in the garden and talked to them. One day, Eve and then Adam sinned by listening to the tempter, Satan, and chose to disobey God. When they did, their relationship with God changed—it was marred by sin and death. Sin and death stood between them and God. God offered hope, though, that one day sin and death would be overcome. It would no longer stand between God and people.

Adam and Eve were put out of the garden. Adam had to toil in pain as he worked the earth. Eve conceived and gave birth to children. Their son, Cain, turned against his brother, Abel, and killed him. Cain suffered unpleasant consequences at the hand of God because of what he had done. He cried out to the Lord saying, "My punishment is more than I can bear."[141] And yet, Cain did bear it and went on to marry and have a family.

Eve gave birth to another son, Seth, who also married and had children.

The number of people on the earth increased. Wickedness, violence and the evil in people's hearts also increased to the point that God was grieved and decided to

---

[141] Genesis 4:13

destroy all living creatures on the earth with a flood. A man named Noah found favor in God's eyes, and God wanted to save him and his immediate family. He told Noah to build an ark or large boat. In it God saved Noah, his family and some of the animals from the flood that covered the earth.

When the flood was gone, and everyone came out of the ark, God made a covenant with Noah and every living creature. He said he would never again destroy all life with a flood, and he put a rainbow in the sky to remind himself of that promise.

After the number of people on earth had increased, God spoke to a man named Abram. He told him to leave his people and his land and go to a land that God would show him. Abram obeyed God and followed him wherever he led. God made a covenant with Abram and his descendants. He said that all people would be blessed through Abram. Along with that covenant, God changed Abram's name to Abraham. He said to Abraham,

> "I will establish my covenant as an everlasting covenant between me and you and your descendants after you for the generations to come, to be your God and the God of your descendants after you. The whole land of Canaan, where you are now an alien, I will give as an everlasting possession to you and your descendants after you; and I will be their God."[142]

Abraham's wife, Sarah, was well past the age of childbearing and had given Abraham no children. And yet, God offered them hope when he said Sarah would still give birth to a son. Just as God had said, Sarah gave birth to Isaac. Isaac married and had twin sons, Jacob and Esau.

---

[142] Genesis 17:7-8

Jacob, later called Israel, had twelve sons. They became known as the Israelites, the descendants of Abraham, his son Isaac and his grandson Jacob. These were the people to whom God intended to give the land he had first promised to Abraham.

Jacob loved his son Joseph more than he did his other sons. Because of that, his brothers hated him and became jealous of him. Eventually, they had the opportunity to get rid of Joseph. They sold him to some merchants who were passing by, and the merchants took him to Egypt. There Joseph became a slave in the house of Potiphar, an Egyptian official. God gave him success in everything he did, and he found favor with Potiphar. He put Joseph in charge of his household, and God blessed Potiphar's household. Eventually, Joseph was unjustly accused of a wrongdoing, and Potiphar put him in prison with the king's prisoners. Even there, God showed his love for Joseph. The prison warden was pleased with Joseph and put him in charge of the prisoners.

Joseph was later released from prison when he was the only person in the land who could tell the king, Pharaoh, what he had dreamed and what the dreams meant. He told Pharaoh that his dreams meant there would be seven years of plenty in the land followed by seven years of famine. Joseph suggested that Pharaoh find a man who would see the country successfully through those years.

Pharaoh considered Joseph to be very discerning and wise, and so he put Joseph in charge of the palace and all of Egypt. Pharaoh said all the people were to submit to Joseph. He also said to Joseph, "Only with respect to the throne will I be greater than you."[143]

---

[143] Genesis 41:40-41

When the famine spread through the land, Egypt was prepared. People from other countries came to Egypt to buy grain.

One day some men came before Joseph to buy grain, and he recognized them as his brothers. They did not recognize him, though. When Joseph finally revealed himself to his brothers, they were terrified. Joseph told them not to be angry with themselves over what they had done to him. He assured them it was all part of God's plan. There was a reason for what Joseph had been through in Egypt. He said, "But God sent me ahead of you to preserve for you a remnant on earth and to save your lives by a great deliverance. So then it was not you who sent me here, but God."[144]

Joseph's entire family moved to Egypt so they could be provided for throughout the rest of the famine. Seventeen years later, Jacob died. With their father dead, Joseph's brothers were afraid Joseph would pay them back for all the ways they had wronged him. They asked Joseph to forgive them and offered themselves to him as his slaves. He reassured them, telling them again that it was all part of God's plan and that he would still provide for them.

After Joseph and his brothers died, a new king or Pharaoh decided to enslave the Israelites because they had become so numerous. They were oppressed more and more with forced labor. But the more they were oppressed, the more numerous they became. The king even went so far as to tell the midwives to kill the Israelite's baby boys as soon as they were born. That didn't work, and so, Pharaoh said that every boy born had to be thrown into the Nile River.

One mother was determined to save her baby boy. She hid him in a basket by the bank of the Nile River. There among

[144] Genesis 45:7-8

the reeds, Pharaoh's daughter found the baby and decided to let him live. She left him with his mother for a while longer. Then he ended up living as the son of Pharaoh's daughter, and she named him Moses. Scripture says, "By faith Moses, when he had grown up, refused to be known as the son of Pharaoh's daughter. He chose to be mistreated along with the people of God rather than to enjoy the pleasures of sin for a short time."[145] As an adult, he went out to watch his people, the Israelites, working and saw an Egyptian beating one of the Israelites or Hebrews. He killed the Egyptian while defending the slave who was being beaten. Pharaoh found out about it and tried to kill Moses. Moses quickly left the area.

Meanwhile, the oppression continued; the slave masters were cruel and ruthlessly demanding. Broken and possibly feeling hopeless, the Israelites finally cried out for help. God heard their cries concerning their slavery and was concerned about them. He remembered his covenant with Abraham, Isaac and Jacob, and so, he sent them help.

God appeared to Moses in the land of Midian to which he had fled. God spoke to Moses from a burning bush, saying, "The cry of the Israelites has reached me, and I have seen the way the Egyptians are oppressing them. So now, go. I am sending you to Pharaoh to bring my people the Israelites out of Egypt."[146]

Moses tried to get out of what God had called him to do, but God finally convinced him that he, with God's help and the help of his brother Aaron, could do the job. Moses knew it was only because of God that he could do the job God had given him, the job of leading God's people out of Egypt. It was later said of him, "By faith he left Egypt, not fearing the king's anger; he persevered because he saw him who is invisible."[147]

[145] Hebrews 11:24-25
[146] Exodus 3:9-10
[147] Hebrews 11:27

Moses and Aaron returned to Egypt and went to the elders of the Israelites. With God's help in doing some miracles, Moses convinced the people that God had indeed seen them and their misery.[148] He had sent help for his people. And the elders bowed down and worshipped God.

When Moses first approached Pharaoh about letting his people go, Pharaoh responded by significantly increasing the Israelites' workload. When the people could not keep up, they were beaten. The elders came to Moses to complain, and when Moses went to God, God told him that Pharaoh would let them go. And it would be because of God's power and might. He would do something that would persuade Pharaoh to finally let the Israelites go.

After God inflicted ten plagues on the Egyptians, the last of which included the death of Pharaoh's firstborn son, Pharaoh was finally convinced. Then God used Moses to lead his people out of Egypt. God parted the waters of the Red Sea so his people could cross on dry land. He closed the waters when the Egyptians reached them, and their army was completely destroyed. God led his people away from the cruelty and oppression of Egypt and toward the land he had promised to Abraham, Isaac, Jacob and their descendants. The people missed the things they had eaten in Egypt and started complaining. God heard their grumbling and provided them with food and water.

They reached the Desert of Sinai and camped in front of Mount Sinai. There God spoke to Moses saying,

> "'You yourselves have seen what I did to Egypt, and how I carried you on eagles' wings and brought you to myself. Now if you obey me fully and keep my covenant, then out of all nations you will be my treasured possession. Although the whole earth is

[148] Exodus 4:29-31

82

mine, you will be for me a kingdom of priests and a holy nation.' These are the words you are to speak to the Israelites."[149]

God gave the Ten Commandments and the rest of his law to Moses. The law covered many things. It told how to deal with sin and keep peace among the people. It included laws about how they were to worship God. It emphasized justice, mercy and doing good.

As God gave the law, he often referred to himself as the "Lord your God, who brought you out of Egypt." He instituted the annual Passover and the Feast of Unleavened Bread to commemorate their deliverance from Egypt. He referred to their time in Egypt as a reason for giving certain laws. Examples of that are:

> "Do not oppress an alien; you yourselves know how it feels to be aliens, because you were aliens in Egypt."[150]

> "And you are to love those who are aliens, for you yourselves were aliens in Egypt."[151]

> "If a fellow Hebrew, a man or a woman, sells himself to you and serves you six years, in the seventh year you must let him go free. And when you release him, do not send him away empty-handed. Supply him liberally from your flock, your threshing floor and your winepress. Give to him as the LORD your God has blessed you. Remember that you were slaves in Egypt and the LORD your God redeemed you.

[149] Exodus 19:4-6
[150] Exodus 23:9
[151] Deuteronomy 10:19

That is why I give you this command today."[152]

"Do not deprive the alien or the fatherless of justice or take the cloak of the widow as a pledge. Remember that you were slaves in Egypt and the LORD your God redeemed you from there. That is why I command you to do this."[153]

"When you are harvesting in your field and you overlook a sheaf, do not go back to get it. Leave it for the alien, the fatherless and the widow, so that the LORD your God may bless you in all the work of your hands. When you beat the olives from your trees, do not go over the branches a second time. Leave what remains for the alien, the fatherless and the widow. When you harvest the grapes in your vineyard, do not go over the vines again. Leave what remains for the alien, the fatherless and the widow. Remember that you were slaves in Egypt. That is why I command you to do this."[154]

"The alien living with you must be treated as one of your native-born. Love him as yourself, for you were aliens in Egypt. I am the LORD your God."[155]

"Because the Israelites are my servants, whom I brought out of Egypt, they must not be sold as slaves. Do not rule over them ruthlessly but fear your God." [156]

[152] Deuteronomy 15:12-15
[153] Deuteronomy 24:17-18
[154] Deuteronomy 24:19-22
[155] Leviticus 19:34
[156] Leviticus 25:42-43

God impressed upon his people again and again that they were to remember their time of oppression and slavery in Egypt. And they were to remember that it was God who delivered them from Egypt and from slavery. They were to remember it as they dealt with other people and as they celebrated their God.

God also impressed upon his people again and again through the years the importance of obeying the laws he was giving them. He enumerated wonderful blessings that would be theirs if they obeyed his commands. He said their enemies would be defeated, their crops would flourish, and they would be established as a holy people. They would have enough for themselves and plenty to share. There would be peace in the land. God would dwell among them and be their God. They would be his people—his treasured possession. They would be a holy nation.

God also told of many disasters that would come upon them if they disobeyed him. He said he would bring upon them terror, diseases and fever. Their crops would fail. He would send wild animals against them, and they would not have food. They would be oppressed and robbed. Later, God promised his people that if they didn't obey him, "you will have nothing but cruel oppression all your days."[157] He said their enemies would overtake them and they would be scattered among other nations.

God said that if, after they disobey him, they confess their sin and humble themselves, he would remember his covenant with them and would remember the land. He would not destroy them completely

If the people chose obedience, they were also choosing the blessings. If they chose to disobey, they were also

---

[157] Deuteronomy 28:33

choosing to have the disasters come upon them. The choice was theirs.

Moses told the people all that God had said to him on Mount Sinai. God had also told them to build a tabernacle as a sanctuary for him. They built it according to the pattern God gave Moses. God's Glory filled it, and the people made sacrifices there. Whenever the people moved from one place to another, they disassembled the tabernacle and took it with them.

When the Israelites left Mount Sinai, they traveled on toward Canaan, the land God had promised them. Upon arriving there, men were sent in to explore the land. They reported to the Israelites that the people who lived there were larger and stronger than they. Only two men, Joshua and Caleb, gave a good report concerning the land. They said that if God were pleased with them, he would lead them into the land and give it to them. After all, they said, "...the Lord is with us. Do not be afraid of them."[158]

The people did not believe Joshua and Caleb's report and even wanted to stone them. The people rebelled against God and were afraid. As a result, God said they would wander in the wilderness for forty years. All the people twenty years of age and older, except Joshua and Caleb, would die during that forty years. God said the people who rebelled would not enter the promised land.

They set out, beginning forty years of wandering in the wilderness. They complained and quarreled because there was not water for the people. And so, God provided water for them. As they traveled, some countries denied them passage through their lands, and they attacked the Israelites. When the Israelites stayed among other people, the people invited them to worship false gods. When the

---

[158] Numbers 14:9

Israelites worshipped those gods, God was angry and punished them. Still, he continued to be with them.

All those who had been twenty years old and older when the Israelites had first reached the promised land died during the wilderness wanderings with the exception of Joshua, Caleb and Moses. God told Moses to begin taking possession of the promised land. He said, "This very day I will begin to put the terror and fear of you on all the nations under heaven. They will hear reports of you and will tremble and be in anguish because of you."[159] And so the Israelites defeated two different kings and took possession of their lands.

Finally, hundreds of years after the promise was first made to Abraham, his descendants were entering the land God had promised them. For centuries, the Israelites had anticipated this. After all this time of waiting, God was fulfilling the promise. He had never forgotten his promise or his people.

God told Moses he would not enter the promised land because he had disobeyed God in the wilderness and had not honored him as holy. Before his death, Moses commissioned Joshua to take his place as leader of the Israelites. He told him, "You have seen with your own eyes all that the LORD your God has done to these two kings. The LORD will do the same to all the kingdoms over there where you are going. Do not be afraid of them; the LORD your God himself will fight for you."[160] Moses also reminded the people of all the laws God had given them. He reminded them that God would be with them. He told them to remember how rebellious they had been since leaving Egypt. As he had done previously, he reminded them to fear God, to love him and to serve him with all their heart and soul. He admonished them to remember God's words to them and to teach them to their children. He

[159] Deuteronomy 2:25
[160] Deuteronomy 3:21-22

reminded them of the blessings that would come to them if they obeyed God and of the disasters that would come upon them if they chose to disobey him.

Moses told them that God also promised that if, after disobeying him, the people turn back to him and obey him with all their heart and soul, he would have compassion on them and gather them from the nations where they would be scattered. He would bring them back to the land that was promised to Abraham, Isaac and Jacob. He would make them successful and more prosperous than before. And God would again delight in them.

In considering who God is and what he had done for his people since he had created them, Moses said to the people, "Has any god ever tried to take for himself one nation out of another nation, by testings, by miraculous signs and wonders, by war, by a mighty hand and an outstretched arm, or by great and awesome deeds, like all the things the Lord your God did for you in Egypt before your very eyes?"[161]

Finally Moses said,

> "See, I set before you today life and prosperity, death and destruction. For I command you today to love the LORD your God, to walk in his ways, and to keep his commands, decrees and laws; then you will live and increase, and the LORD your God will bless you in the land you are entering to possess. But if your heart turns away and you are not obedient, and if you are drawn away to bow down to other gods and worship them, I declare to you this day that you will certainly be destroyed. You will not live long in the land you are crossing the

[161] Deuteronomy 4:34

Jordan to enter and possess. This day I call heaven and earth as witnesses against you that I have set before you life and death, blessings and curses. Now choose life, so that you and your children may live and that you may love the LORD your God, listen to his voice, and hold fast to him. For the LORD is your life, and he will give you many years in the land he swore to give to your fathers, Abraham, Isaac and Jacob."[162]

Soon after that, Moses climbed Mount Nebo. From there, God showed Moses the land he had promised to his people. Then Moses died and was buried.

God parted the waters of the Jordan River so that his people could cross it on dry land. Joshua led them as they conquered city after city and defeated one king after another. They experienced victory after victory because God was fighting for them.

God had Joshua divide the land among the tribes of Israel. Moses had allotted some of the land to two tribes before he died. Now Joshua divided the rest among the other Israelite tribes as God had commanded through Moses.

When Joshua grew old, he called together all the tribes of Israel and spoke to them. He reminded them of what God had done for them and admonished them to serve the Lord faithfully. He reminded them that if they chose to serve foreign gods, the Lord their God would bring disaster on them. And Joshua died.

Israel served God during Joshua's lifetime and the lifetime of the elders who outlived him. Then a generation of people grew up who did not know God, and they did evil. They worshipped the gods of the people around them, and

[162] Deuteronomy 30:15-20

God became angry. He handed them over to their enemies just as he had said he would do if they disobeyed him.

When the people groaned under the oppression of their enemies, God raised up a judge to save them "for the LORD had compassion on them as they groaned under those who oppressed and afflicted them."[163] When the judge died, the people again turned away from God and served other gods.

God decided it was time to no longer drive out any of the nations that were left in the land he had promised to his people. And so...the oppression began again. And the cycle repeated itself. For over three hundred years this happened again and again. Each time after enduring years of oppression at the hand of their enemies, God's people would cry out to him for help, and he would raise up a judge to deliver them. And each time after the judge died, the people would again turn away from God. And yet, again and again, God raised up judges to save his people from the oppression.

It was during this time that a woman named Hannah lived. Having children was very important to the Israelites, and Hannah had not been able to have any. When she and her husband went to worship at Shiloh, Hannah asked God for a son. Crying and in anguish, she said that if he gave her one, she would give him to the Lord all the days of his life. God did give her a son and she named him Samuel. While he was very young, she took him to live and serve at the house of the Lord at Shiloh. Samuel became a prophet and judge for Israel. When he grew old, he appointed his sons to be judges after him. His sons were dishonest and perverted justice, so Israel complained that they did not want them to be judges.

[163] Judges 2:18

Instead, the Israelites asked for a king to lead them. God had known they would ask for a king, and he wanted to choose for them the kind of king they needed.[164] That kind of king would not want things that would turn his heart from God. He would not accumulate horses, wives, gold and silver. He would write by hand a copy of God's law, keep it with him and read it all the days of his life so that he could honor God, live obediently and not think he's better than the people he serves as king.

God listened to the people and had Samuel warn them of what it would be like to be under a king. Samuel told the people that they would be servants of the king and that he would take their sons and daughters, their servants and the best of their fields, olive groves, vineyards and livestock. He said to the people, "When that day comes, you will cry out for relief from the king you have chosen, and the LORD will not answer you in that day."[165]

Still, the people wanted a king—one who would rule them and go before them into battle. They wanted a king who would make them like the other nations.

Samuel anointed a young man named Saul that God had chosen to be king. Saul eventually became disobedient to God, and God was sorry he had made him king. Samuel told Saul that God had chosen another man—a man after God's own heart—to be king in Saul's place.

Samuel anointed the man God had chosen; he anointed David, a young man and a shepherd, as king of Israel. The Spirit of the Lord left Saul and came powerfully upon David from that day forward, but Saul continued to act as king.

David, meanwhile, began to serve Saul as a harp player while also taking care of his father's sheep. David was described as a warrior and a brave man, though, and when

[164] Deuteronomy 17:14-20
[165] 1 Samuel 8:18

the Israelites were threatened by a Philistine "giant" who had spent his life fighting, David stepped forward and offered to fight him. Goliath came against David with a sword, a spear, a javelin and many years of fighting experience. David said he came against Goliath "in the name of the Lord Almighty."[166] Using only David's slingshot and a stone, God gave young David victory over Goliath. Afterwards, David fought in Saul's army and, based on his success, Saul gave him a high position in his army. Because of David's continued success and how pleased the people were with him, Saul became angry and jealous of him. He was also afraid of David because the Lord was with him and not with Saul.

For the rest of Saul's life, he and David were enemies.[167] Driven by his fear, anger and jealousy, Saul was continually trying to find David and kill him. Again and again, David escaped from Saul. Still, Saul pursued him. Saul even killed those who helped David. He struck out at his own son to kill him because he believed his son had sided with David against Saul. Another time, he had eighty-five priests of the Lord killed. He also had all the people living in the same town as the priests killed, and all because they had helped David by not reporting his whereabouts to Saul.

A couple of times David stood close enough to Saul to kill him without him knowing it. Despite that, David would not kill him, saying that he could not lift his hand against the Lord's anointed. The second time he spared Saul's life, he said, "'Don't destroy him! Who can lay a hand on the Lord's anointed and be guiltless? As surely as the LORD lives,' he said, 'the LORD himself will strike him; either his time will come, and he will die, or he will go into battle and perish. But the LORD forbid that I should lay a hand on the Lord's anointed.'"[168]

[166] 1 Samuel 17:45
[167] 1 Samuel 18:29
[168] 1 Samuel 26:9-11

Saul and his three sons ended up dying in battle. Saul's head was cut off and his body was hung on a wall.

The men of Judah then anointed David king. Even then, David showed respect for Saul's position by blessing the men who had so kindly taken down the bodies of Saul and his sons and buried them.

The strife was not over yet, though. Another of Saul's sons was made king over Israel. A war began between Saul's people and David's people that lasted a long time. But eventually, David was made king by all the tribes of Israel. Serving as king and warrior for Israel, David conquered many nations and became famous. Even then, he wanted to show kindness to the house of Saul because of his friendship with one of Saul's sons. Saul had a grandson who still lived, and David restored to him all the land that had belonged to Saul and granted him the privilege of always eating at King David's table.

David was a shepherd, a harp player, a warrior and a king. He was the author of many psalms, some of which are praises to God for his part in David's life and the life of the Israelites. David was a man after God's own heart.

As all people are, David was a sinner. He committed adultery with a lady named Bathsheba and plotted the murder of her husband. After the man was killed, David took Bathsheba as his wife. God was displeased with what David had done. As a result of David's sin, the child Bathsheba had conceived by him died. God later blessed them with another son, whom they named Solomon.

Even with all the trials in David's life, he wrote, "But you, O Lord, are a compassionate and gracious God, slow to anger, abounding in love and faithfulness."[169] He also

---

[169] Psalm 86:15

wrote, "Your love, O Lord, reaches to the heavens, your faithfulness to the skies. Your righteousness is like the mighty mountains, your justice like the great deep. O Lord, you preserve both man and beast. How priceless is your unfailing love! Both high and low among men find refuge in the shadow of your wings."[170] David knew God had all these qualities, and no matter what was happening in David's life, he knew he could rely on God.

David and Bathsheba's son, Solomon, succeeded David as king. As God had promised David, Israel lived in peace during Solomon's life. Also, as God had promised David, Solomon built the temple of God in Jerusalem.

After Solomon's death, his son Rehoboam became king. The people rebelled against him and the kingdom of Israel divided. Rehoboam ruled Judah, the southern kingdom, and a man named Jeroboam ruled the northern kingdom, Israel.

Jereboam, the first king of Israel, presented the people with golden calves who he said were their gods who had brought them out of Egypt. He established places of worship in Israel so the people would not travel to Jerusalem to worship as God had commanded them. He made priests of people who were not from the tribe of Levi, and in doing that, he disobeyed God's commands. He broke many of the commands concerning worship. God tried to get Jeroboam to change his wicked ways, but he would not. Because of his sins and those he led Israel to commit, Jeroboam had provoked God to anger.

Jeroboam set the stage for the kings who succeeded him. One of the kings who succeeded him "did evil in the eyes of the Lord, walking in the ways of Jeroboam and in his sin which he had caused Israel to commit."[171] In the same

---

[170] Psalm 36:5-7
[171] 1 Kings 15:34

way, other kings who came after Jeroboam were compared to him because of the evil they did.

It was a time of war and oppression for God's people. Fighting occurred between Israel and Judah as well as with other nations. God's people suffered famine and lack of rain. They suffered oppression repeatedly at the hand of their enemies.

God sent prophets to his people to warn them to abandon their wicked ways and false gods and return to him, the true God. The prophets emphasized obedience to God and serving only him with their whole heart. They also told about a Deliverer whom God would send to the people.

The prophet Elijah came up against Israel's King Ahab and his wife, Jezebel. Ahab, strongly influenced by his wife, did more evil than any of the kings before him. For one thing, he and his wife served and worshipped Baal, a false god. Ahab even built a temple to Baal.

Part of God's response to Ahab's sin was to withhold rain from the land so that there was a severe famine in Israel. God eventually told Elijah to go before Ahab because he was going to send rain again. Elijah, who thought he was the only prophet not yet killed by Jezebel, arranged a contest between the prophets of Baal and Elijah.[172] Elijah wanted Israel to see who the true God was and choose whom they would worship. The contest began, and Baal never responded to the long and loud cries of his worshippers even though they went on for hours. When it was Elijah's turn to call on God, he prayed that the people would know that the Lord is God and that he was turning the hearts of his people back to him. God responded immediately. The people fell down and worshipped God. The prophets of Baal were gathered together and killed. And Elijah told Ahab that God would again send rain.

[172] 1 Kings 18:19-40

Meanwhile, Jezebel, in her anger over the deaths of Baal's prophets, went after Elijah. Elijah ran and hid because of his fear. After a while, God revealed to Elijah that he was not the only person still alive that continued to be faithful to God. There were still seven thousand Israelites who had not turned away from God to worship Baal.

Eventually, King Ahab was killed in battle, and then, after Jezebel's death, what happened to her body fulfilled what Elijah had prophesied about her.[173]

Elisha was another well-known prophet to Israel. He was anointed by Elijah to take over for him as prophet. He finished the work started by Elijah in getting rid of Baal worship and destroying the family of King Ahab. Elisha showed compassion to people by doing miracles that reminded them of God's power and presence. In obedience to God, he anointed Jehu as king, and Jehu was responsible for killing all the ministers, priests and prophets of Baal at that time. He also destroyed the sacred pillar and the temple of Baal.

Hosea was another prophet to Israel. Using the example of marriage to an unfaithful wife, Hosea's message revolved around God's continuing love for an unfaithful nation. He talked about Israel's sin and unfaithfulness to God as well as Israel's disregard for God. He told them their sins had been their downfall. He said the people, "Do not cry out to me from their hearts but wail upon their beds."[174] He called the people to turn from their evil ways and return wholeheartedly to God who loves them. He offered them hope when he talked about God's love for them and said the people would come back to him and he would settle them in their land again.

Many more prophets were sent with the difficult and sometimes dangerous job of warning Israel and

[173] 2 Kings 9:36-37
[174] Hosea 7:14

encouraging them to leave their idolatry and sin and return to God. They were sent to people not willing to listen. All of this happened in the context of being repeatedly attacked by Judah and other nations. Still, the people didn't give up their sinful ways, and the northern kingdom, Israel, was eventually taken captive by Assyria. And, as God had said through his prophets, many Israelites were exiled to far away lands.

Like Israel, Judah had many kings who did evil, kings who sinned and stirred up God's jealous anger. Many kings did not devote their hearts fully to God. They built pagan shrines and altars to Baal and some offered their sons in fire to pagan gods. They worshipped the starry hosts. In all the evil the kings did, they also led the people of Judah to sin right along with them.

Mixed in among the evil kings were those who did what was right and pleasing to God. They were responsible for ridding the country of idols and things related to idol worship, especially worship of Baal. Some even reinstituted worshipping God.

King Joash repaired the temple that had been damaged and neglected. He had it restored it to its original design and even strengthened it. Later in his life, though, Joash began to follow the advice of ungodly leaders in Judah.[175] He turned from God and began worshipping idols. God became angry but still sent prophets to turn the people back to him. The people didn't listen, and so God delivered them into the hand of their enemies who killed their leaders and plundered their land.

Another king in Judah, Hezekiah, "trusted in the Lord, the God of Israel. There was no one like him among all the kings of Judah, either before him or after him. He held fast to the Lord and did not cease to follow him; he kept the

---

[175] 2 Chronicles 24:17-23

commands the Lord had given Moses."[176] He sought help from God's prophet, Isaiah, when threatened by the king of Assyria; he asked Isaiah to pray for the remnant of God's people.[177] Isaiah prayed, and God defeated the Assyrians.

King Josiah was very young when he began seeking God. He rid Judah and Jerusalem of all evidence of idolatrous worship. He was having repair work done on the temple when the Book of the Law was found. It was read aloud, and Josiah tore his robes, humbling himself before God. God said that, because of Josiah's response, he would let him live in peace and not have to see the disaster that would happen to Jerusalem and Judah. Then Josiah, along with the people and priests, renewed the covenant to follow the Lord and live obediently. He ordered that the Passover be celebrated. "Neither before nor after Josiah was there a king like him who turned to the Lord as he did—with all his heart and with all his soul and with all his strength, in accordance with all the Law of Moses."[178]

After Josiah, the kings of Judah were evil. The people tended to follow the king when it came to spirituality and worship. God still loved the people and wanted them to turn from their evil ways. Instead of the turmoil and disaster that came with not seeking God and instead of the attacks they were experiencing from other nations, God wanted to bless them richly.

God sent prophet after prophet to warn them of what was to come because of their disobedience. He, through Isaiah, pronounced judgment on Judah and Israel. Isaiah talked about those who had attacked Judah and about God's people turning on each other. He told of the future defeat of both Assyria and Babylon. And he offered hope for the remnant of his people when he talked about the deliverance and restoration of Israel; some captives would

[176] 2 Kings 18:5-6
[177] 2 Kings 19:2-4
[178] 2 Kings 23:25

return to their homes in Israel. He also prophesied about the coming Messiah or Deliverer.

Joel was a prophet with a message for Judah, the southern kingdom. His message was short but powerful. It communicated judgment and also hope. He described a terrible invasion of locusts that would devastate the land, destroy the crops and even invade the homes of the people. He said that is how God's punishment can be. Joel then said, "'Even now,' declares the Lord, 'return to me with all your heart, with fasting and weeping and mourning. Rend your heart and not your garments. Return to the Lord your God, for he is gracious and compassionate, slow to anger and abounding in love, and he relents from sending calamity.'"[179] Joel said that after the people turn back to God, he would take pity on them and bless them abundantly. He would even pour out his Spirit on them, and all who call on the Lord's name would be saved.

Jeremiah had a very trying job as prophet. He was accused of being a deserter and was arrested, beaten, put in stocks and thrown into prison. Later, he was thrown into a cistern where he could have starved to death if it weren't for some men who rescued him. He was also threatened with death for prophesying. He was ridiculed, mocked and insulted. Because of the idolatrous worship, Jeremiah pronounced judgment on God's people and on the remnant that had fled to Egypt instead of staying in Jerusalem. Jeremiah felt the burden of the people's sin, and he bravely confronted them about it. He told them, "Consider then and realize how evil and bitter it is for you when you forsake the Lord your God..."[180]

Jeremiah also told of God's plans to give his people hope. Speaking for God, he said, "For I know the plans I have for you...plans to prosper you and not to harm you, plans to

[179] Joel 2:12-14
[180] Jeremiah 2:19

give you a hope and a future."[181] He went on to say that when the people seek God with their whole heart, they would find him, and he would bring them back to the land he had promised to them. He told about the coming restoration of Jerusalem with healing, rebuilding, cleansing, forgiving, abundant prosperity and peace. He spoke of a new covenant that God would make with his people.

If God's people continued to disobey him and his commands, they were certain to face captivity and oppression by their captors. Still, the people didn't obey and finally, long after the Assyrians had taken Israel captive, Judah fell into the hands of the Babylonians. They were taken captive and, like Israel, they were exiled to foreign lands. Their enemies destroyed the temple and the wall around Jerusalem.

Many years later, after Cyrus and the Persians had defeated the Babylonians, God fulfilled a prophecy made through Jeremiah.[182] He moved Cyrus to commit to the building of the temple in Jerusalem, seeing that supplies were provided for doing that and even returning some of the articles that had been removed earlier from the temple by the king of Babylon. Cyrus allowed some of the captives to return to Jerusalem where they rebuilt the altar, offered sacrifices to God on it and then began rebuilding the temple of God. Even with opposition and delays, the temple of God was finally rebuilt.

A later king of Persia, Artaxerxes, commissioned Ezra, a priest and teacher of God's laws, to return to Jerusalem taking with him a second group of exiles.[183] He was given access to money from the royal treasury to secure things needed for the temple of God, and because of his wisdom, he was also to appoint magistrates and judges who knew

[181] Jeremiah 29:11
[182] Jeremiah 25:11-12; 29:10-14
[183] Ezra 7:11-26

God's laws to help rule the people. Ezra was quite distraught over the sin of the Israelite people including the priests and Levites and confronted them concerning it. The people wept bitterly and repented, separating themselves from their foreign wives and their children by those wives. They set themselves apart for God as he desired.

Artaxerxes also sent Nehemiah, accompanied by army officers and cavalry for protection, to Jerusalem. There Nehemiah and the people worked to rebuild the wall around Jerusalem. Even with opposition, the wall was completed in only fifty-two days; that is because it had been done with the help of the God of the Israelites. Knowing that, the surrounding nations became frightened.

As bleak as the lives of the prophets and the Israelites may have been at times, God always offered them hope. Most immediate were the blessings that would come with obedience and loving God wholeheartedly. In the more distant future was the hope of restoring Israel to the promised land and the rebuilding of Jerusalem and the temple of God. Even further in the future was the hope of the coming Messiah.

The word of God's prophets proved to be true. The hope God had promised was being realized by his people. God's people had been taken captive by other nations and had been exiled to foreign lands. They suffered at the hands of their captors. And true to his word, God brought them back to the land he had promised to Abraham, Isaac, Jacob and their descendants. He was even restoring the Temple of God and Jerusalem, the city where God had chosen to put his name.[184]

God's prophets had also spoken of the hope of a Messiah, Deliverer and Savior who was yet to come. The Messiah would be of the seed of Abraham and David. His

---

[184] 1 Kings 11:36

punishment would bring much wanted peace to God's people. But it would still be about four hundred years before God's promise of a Deliverer would be fulfilled.

Even after waiting so many years, people still knew of and expected the Messiah and Deliverer God had promised. Hope was still alive. And then...

In the small town of Bethlehem, a baby was born to a couple. The mother, Mary, was a virgin whom God had chosen. The Holy Spirit had come upon her, and the Most High had overshadowed her so that she became pregnant. The baby was to be called Jesus and the Son of God. Mary's husband, Joseph, was a man who bravely married her, knowing he was not the father of the baby. An angel had visited each of them individually and told them how Mary would conceive.

When it was time for Mary and Joseph to take the baby Jesus to the temple, there were two people who were especially glad to see him. The Holy Spirit had reassured Simeon that he would see the Lord's Messiah (Christ) before he died. Simeon recognized the baby Jesus for who he was and praised God. He said Jesus would be a light to the Gentiles and glory for God's people, the Israelites. Anna, a prophetess, was also at the temple and told everybody, those who had been looking forward to Jerusalem finally being redeemed, about the baby Jesus.

Jesus "grew and became strong; he was filled with wisdom and the grace of God was upon him."[185] He also "grew in wisdom and stature, and in favor with God and man."[186]

When Jesus was grown, he traveled around and talked much about God and his kingdom. The religious leaders living then had interpreted and distorted God's laws so much that people were not living the way God had

---

[185] Luke 2:40
[186] Luke 2:52

intended. Jesus was calling people back to a way of believing, living, acting and relating to others that was pleasing to God. The focus had been taken off God and was instead on trying to live up to what the religious leaders demanded of the people. Jesus even taught using the phrase, "You have heard it was said... But I tell you."[187] He used Old Testament commandments or the people's understanding of them as examples to show what was really important. What mattered wasn't just doing the minimum expected but taking that expectation to heart and doing everything they could to live that way.

One example of this is when Jesus said, "You have heard that it was said, 'Love your neighbor and hate your enemy.' But I tell you: Love your enemies and pray for those who persecute you, that you may be sons of your Father in heaven."[188] He explained to the people that they needed to love all people and not just those who would love them back. Jesus told the people they were to love God with their whole being and also love their neighbor as themselves. He later illustrated loving others when he told a story about a man who was traveling from one town to another and on the way, was robbed, stripped, beaten and left for dead. A priest and a Levite, both people of God, each saw the man as they were traveling the same road. First, the priest passed by the beaten man, even going to the other side of the road to avoid him. Then the Levite passed by the man, also going to the other side of the road as he passed him. Finally, a Samaritan traveled the same road. Samaritans were looked down on by the Israelites or Jews. But it was he, instead of the two men of God, who stopped and helped the man who had been left for dead. And he didn't do just the minimum needed. He cleaned and bandaged the wounds. He also put the man on his own donkey, and taking him to an inn, the Samaritan took care of him. The next day, he paid the innkeeper to take care of him. He also said he would return and pay for

[187] Matthew 5:21-22, 27-28, 31-32, 33-34, 38-39, 43-44
[188] Matthew 5:43-45

anything his money would not cover.[189] The Samaritan acted as a true neighbor, showing mercy and love, and Jesus told his followers to go and do as the Samaritan had.

With all that the religious leaders demanded of the people, obedience was not an easy thing. Jesus, on the other hand, talked to the people about many subjects related to pleasing God. He talked much about loving God with our whole being and loving others. He talked about not worrying, how to pray, living in such a way that would point others to God, distinguishing between what was really tradition and what God wanted, causing others to sin, what we owe to civil authorities, forgiveness, faith, giving from the heart and serving. Jesus explained how people could live in obedience. When it came to pleasing God, there was definitely hope for believers.

Jesus engaged his listeners on a personal level when he told parables like the one about the Samaritan helping the man who was robbed, beaten and left for dead. Parables were stories to which people could relate that helped teach them a lesson. They were about things from people's everyday life, things that would have meaning to them. Jesus told many parables that illustrated what the kingdom of God was like.[190] More than once he told parables using examples of people farming to illustrate the kingdom of God. Other examples he used involved a woman mixing yeast into bread, a man finding a treasure hidden in a field and the kind of net used in fishing. He really wanted people to understand about his Father's kingdom.

Jesus also met people where they were and was sensitive to their needs. Many followed Jesus as he traveled about and taught people. Twice the crowds were very large, and they needed to eat. One time there were five thousand men in the crowd, and the other time there were about four

[189] Luke 10:30-37
[190] Matthew 13:1-52

thousand, not including the women and children. When Jesus was with the four thousand, he said, "I have compassion for these people; they have already been with me three days and have nothing to eat. If I send them home hungry, they will collapse on the way, because some of them have come a long distance."[191] Each time, Jesus took the little food they had, gave thanks for it and told his disciples to pass out the food to the people. They did what he told them, and the people ate. After everyone had eaten, each time there were several baskets full of food left over.

When passing through Samaria, Jesus saw a woman at a well. Right away, the woman would normally have had at least two strikes against her. First, she was a Samaritan and second, she was a woman of ill-repute. In addition, a Jewish man would not stop to talk with a Samaritan. Unlike others, Jesus was not concerned about the customary behavior in such a situation. He was tired and wanted a drink of water, and probably of more importance, was that this woman had needs she didn't even realize. Jesus started a conversation in which he told her about living water that would spring up into eternal life. He knew all about her personal life, her life of sin. He knew that she had already had five husbands and was living with a man who was not even her husband. It was when he told her those things that the woman realized God must have sent Jesus. They talked about worship, and Jesus confirmed to the woman that he was the Messiah the people were expecting.

The woman went back to her town and told the people to come see this man who knew everything about her and who might be the Messiah or Christ. Because Jesus talked to this one woman who would normally have been avoided and scorned by most Jews, many people became

---

[191] Mark 8:2-3

believers and were convinced that Jesus really is the Savior sent by God.

Jesus did many things that showed his love and compassion for his people. He raised a twelve-year old girl and a widow's only son from the dead, as well as bringing a friend of his back to life. He healed people—the lame, the blind, those with leprosy, the demon-possessed and many more. Jesus loved and cared about people. He wanted to show them the love that God has for them.

Jesus had twelve men with whom he worked very closely for about three years. When his time to die drew near, Jesus wanted to prepare those disciples. Jesus was going to be arrested and hung on a cross to die. The disciples were going to be scattered, and Jesus didn't want them to lose hope. He promised that his Father would send the Counselor, the Holy Spirit, the Spirit of Truth, to comfort them, teach them everything and remind them of all that Jesus had said to them. He would also testify about Jesus and convict the world of guilt concerning sin, righteousness and judgment. He told them they would soon be scattered, but not to worry about him because he would not be alone; the Father would be with him. He told them these things to prepare them for the events surrounding his arrest, death, burial and resurrection so that they would believe when the things happened as he said. He also told them so they would have peace. Jesus was leaving them with peace, a peace the world could not give them. They would have troubles in this world but Jesus told them to not be afraid because he had overcome the world.

Things did happen just as Jesus had said they would. He was arrested, crucified on a cross, buried in a borrowed tomb and rose from the dead on the third day. After appearing to and talking with many disciples, Jesus ascended into heaven. He sits on a throne there at the right hand of God.

And the Holy Spirit came just as Jesus had said he would. The disciples were gathered together in Jerusalem when the Spirit came on them with power. Many people were completely amazed at the manifestation of the Holy Spirit. The apostle Peter told the people that King David had spoken of the resurrection of the Messiah, the Christ, and that God had raised Jesus from the dead. He also told them they were responsible for crucifying Christ and that God had made Jesus both Lord and Christ. The people's hearts were troubled when they heard that, and they asked what they should do. Peter said to them, "Repent and be baptized, every one of you, in the name of Jesus Christ for the forgiveness of your sins. And you will receive the gift of the Holy Spirit. The promise is for you and your children and for all who are far off—for all whom the Lord our God will call."[192] Many responded to Peter's message and were baptized into Christ.

Jesus' disciples began to spread the word of Jesus, the Messiah. Many people were receptive to their message of hope and salvation. Some people, though, were quite opposed to it. As a result, some believers were arrested, thrown into prison and even killed. And still the good news about Jesus spread.

The apostle Paul wrote many letters to churches to encourage them as they strived to live for Jesus. Paul wrote about severe hardships he and another believer, Timothy, had suffered and said, "Indeed, in our hearts we felt the sentence of death. But this happened that we might not rely on ourselves but on God, who raises the dead. He has delivered us from such a deadly peril, and he will deliver us. On him we have set our hope that he will continue to deliver us..."[193]

Throughout the Bible, God's plan was to restore the relationship between himself and people. From the time

[192] Acts 2:38-39
[193] 2 Corinthians 1:9-10

Adam and Eve first sinned, God has been doing things in the lives of people to turn their hearts to him. Jesus lived in such a way that we might see the Father God through him. Sometimes painful, difficult things happen that drive us to the heart of a compassionate God. He is our hope.

Jesus was the Messiah, the Christ for whom the Israelites or Jews had been waiting. He is the one told about since the time of Adam and Eve. He is the blessing spoken of to Abraham. Moses and David spoke about the coming Messiah. He was the hope of which the prophets spoke. He is the ultimate salvation and deliverance of Israel. He is the ultimate salvation and deliverance for all who choose to call on his name and follow him wholeheartedly. God offers hope now in his promise that Jesus will return to take us to live with him forever.

Hope was fulfilled in many ways throughout the Old Testament. Sometimes, it was having food provided for the hungry. Sometimes, it was realizing that a person's difficult times were all part of God's bigger plan. It was knowing that God had kept his promise to give you a son when you had lost all hope. It was knowing that it was God who had heard your cries for help and cared enough to act on your behalf. It was realizing that God had not only protected your baby but was using your son to deliver your people. It was being rescued from slavery and from your enemies. It was having your only son raised from the dead. It was realizing that God was fulfilling his covenant made with your ancestors long ago, that is, with Abraham, Isaac and Jacob. It was finding out that you weren't the only one still being true to God. It was knowing it was God who had repeatedly rescued you from death as you were doing the job to which he had called you. It was knowing there was still a remnant of God's people. It was having a foreign king give permission and even support your return to Jerusalem. It was having a foreign king provide protection and funding to help you rebuild the temple of God and the wall around Jerusalem. It is when God enables you to persevere when you thought you could not bear any more. It is realizing that God always has been a God of compassion and hope.

When things look bleak and hope is hard to grasp, people can always turn to God who always offers hope. He is passionate about his people. As David said long ago, God is compassionate, gracious, slow to anger, full of unfailing love and faithfulness. All men can find refuge in him. When we seek him with our whole heart, he will draw us to him, and we will find him. Long ago, Moses spoke words that are as relevant now as they were then. He said, "...love the Lord your God, listen to his voice, and hold fast to him. For the Lord is your life."[194]

The apostle Peter wrote, "... it was not with perishable things...that you were redeemed from the empty way of life handed down to you from your forefathers, but with the precious blood of Christ... He was chosen before the creation of the world but was revealed in these last times for your sake. Through him you believe in God, who raised him from the dead and glorified him, and so your faith and hope are in God."[195]

Paul wrote about the "faith and love that spring from the hope that is stored up for you in heaven and that you have already heard about in the word of truth, the gospel that has come to you."[196]

As always, our hope is in God. It is in his son Jesus. It is a hope that will be realized fully when we see Jesus face to face and fall down to worship before the throne of our God.

[194] Deuteronomy 30:20
[195] 1 Peter 1:18-21
[196] Colossians 1:5-6

Questions for Thought

What is your source of hope?

What is there about Jesus—who he is, his life, death, burial, resurrection and ascension into heaven—that would give people hope?

TELLING THE STORY

Throughout the Bible, people told the story of what God had done. Remembering it was very important. One generation told it to the next. Fathers told it to their children, the elders explained it to the people and the prophets reminded the Israelites of it. God reminded the people again and again throughout time of what he had done for them and why he had done it.

When God had brought his people out of Egypt and they had come to Mount Sinai, God delivered his law to the people through Moses. Moses told the people,

> "Only be careful and watch yourselves closely so that you do not forget the things your eyes have seen or let them slip from your heart as long as you live. Teach them to your children and to their children after them."[197]

Concerning the commandments God gave them, Moses said,

> "Hear, O Israel: The LORD our God, the LORD is one. Love the LORD your God with all your heart and with all your soul and with all your strength. These commandments that I give you today are to be upon your hearts. Impress them on your children. Talk about them when you sit at home and when you walk along the road, when you lie down and when you get up. Tie them as symbols on your hands and bind them on your foreheads. Write them on the doorframes of your houses and on your gates."[198]

[197] Deuteronomy 4:9
[198] Deuteronomy 6:4-9

Knowing the hearts of people, God knew that once his people entered the land he had promised to Abraham, Isaac, Jacob and their descendents, the people might forget that it was God who had accomplished that for them. Moses told the people that when they were enjoying its great abundance and good times, they should be careful to not forget that it was the Lord who had delivered them out of Egypt and slavery.

Before Moses died, and when the Israelites were getting ready to enter the land God had promised to give them, Moses admonished the people saying,

> "Remember the days of old; consider the generations long past. Ask your father and he will tell you, your elders, and they will explain to you."[199]

The writer of some of the Psalms said,

> "When I was in distress, I sought the Lord; at night I stretched out untiring hands and my soul refused to be comforted...Then I thought, 'To this I will appeal: the years of the right hand of the Most High.' I will remember the deeds of the LORD; yes, I will remember your miracles of long ago. I will meditate on all your works and consider all your mighty deeds. Your ways, O God, are holy. What god is so great as our God?"[200]

The writer of that Psalm knew the reassurance and comfort he would find in meditating on the things God had done for him and his people. In that, he could find rest for his soul.

---

[199] Deuteronomy 32:7
[200] Psalms 77:2, 10-13

David, who was a shepherd and was chosen by God to be king, wrote many psalms. In them, he shares much of his own life and struggles. Once when David was seeking relief through God's mercy, he wrote,

> "I remember the days of long ago; I meditate on all your works and consider what your hands have done. I spread out my hands to you; my soul thirsts for you like a parched land."[201]

David knew the importance of knowing and dwelling on what God had done for his people. He wrote,

> "I will exalt you, my God the King; I will praise your name for ever and ever. Every day I will praise you and extol your name for ever and ever. Great is the LORD and most worthy of praise; his greatness no one can fathom. One generation will commend your works to another; they will tell of your mighty acts. They will speak of the glorious splendor of your majesty, and I will meditate on your wonderful works. They will tell of the power of your awesome works, and I will proclaim your great deeds. They will celebrate your abundant goodness and joyfully sing of your righteousness."[202]

In one of the psalms, the writer told the story of God making his covenant with Abraham, Isaac and Jacob. He told about Joseph and about Joseph's family ending up in Egypt. He told about how God brought his people out of Egypt and gave them the promised land. By telling that story, he wanted to make known to people what God had done; he wanted to remind them. The Psalmist wrote,

[201] Psalm 143:5-6
[202] Psalm 145:1-7

"Give thanks to the LORD, call on his name; make known among the nations what he has done. Sing to him, sing praise to him; tell of all his wonderful acts. Glory in his holy name; let the hearts of those who seek the LORD rejoice. Look to the LORD and his strength; seek his face always.

Remember the wonders he has done, his miracles, and the judgments he pronounced, O descendants of Abraham his servant, O sons of Jacob, his chosen ones. He is the LORD our God; his judgments are in all the earth.

He remembers his covenant forever, the word he commanded, for a thousand generations, the covenant he made with Abraham, the oath he swore to Isaac. He confirmed it to Jacob as a decree, to Israel as an everlasting covenant: 'To you I will give the land of Canaan as the portion you will inherit.'

When they were but few in number, few indeed, and strangers in it, they wandered from nation to nation, from one kingdom to another. He allowed no one to oppress them; for their sake he rebuked kings: 'Do not touch my anointed ones; do my prophets no harm.'

He called down famine on the land and destroyed all their supplies of food; and he sent a man before them—Joseph, sold as a slave. They bruised his feet with shackles, his neck was put in irons, till what he foretold came to pass, till the word of the LORD proved him true. The king sent and released him, the ruler of peoples set him free. He made him master of his household, ruler over all he possessed, to instruct his princes as he pleased and teach his elders wisdom.

Then Israel entered Egypt; Jacob lived as an alien in the land of Ham. The LORD made his people very fruitful; he made them too numerous for their foes, whose hearts he turned to hate his people, to conspire against his servants. He sent Moses his servant, and Aaron, whom he had chosen. They performed his miraculous signs among them, his wonders in the land of Ham. He sent darkness and made the land dark—for had they not rebelled against his words? He turned their waters into blood, causing their fish to die. Their land teemed with frogs, which went up into the bedrooms of their rulers. He spoke, and there came swarms of flies, and gnats throughout their country. He turned their rain into hail, with lightning throughout their land; he struck down their vines and fig trees and shattered the trees of their country. He spoke, and the locusts came, grasshoppers without number; they ate up every green thing in their land, ate up the produce of their soil. Then he struck down all the firstborn in their land, the firstfruits of all their manhood.

He brought out Israel, laden with silver and gold, and from among their tribes no one faltered. Egypt was glad when they left, because dread of Israel had fallen on them. He spread out a cloud as a covering, and a fire to give light at night. They asked, and he brought them quail and satisfied them with the bread of heaven. He opened the rock, and water gushed out; like a river it flowed in the desert.

For he remembered his holy promise given to his servant Abraham. He brought out his people with rejoicing, his chosen ones with shouts of joy; he gave them the lands of the nations, and they fell heir to what others had toiled for—that they might keep his precepts and observe his laws. Praise the LORD."[203]

As God's people spoke about him, they also remembered him as Creator, and told what he had done. The prophet Jeremiah when comparing the false gods to the LORD, the true God, said to the people,

"But God made the earth by his power; he founded the world by his wisdom and stretched out the heavens by his understanding. When he thunders, the waters in the heavens roar; he makes clouds rise from the ends of the earth. He sends lightning with the rain and brings out the wind from his storehouses."[204]

The prophet Nehemiah lived during and following the captivity of God's people by the Assyrians and Babylonians. He and some of the people returned to Jerusalem and rebuilt the wall around the city. When it was completed,[205] he said the people gathered together, and Ezra, the priest and scribe, read the Book of the Law of Moses[206] to the people. The people wept as they listened attentively to the words. Nehemiah, Ezra and the Levites told the people not to grieve though. They said that day

[203] Psalm 105:2-45
[204] Jeremiah 10:12-13
[205] Nehemiah 6:15
[206] Nehemiah 8:1-3

was sacred to the Lord and that the joy of the Lord was their strength. The people understood and went away to celebrate joyfully.

Later that same month, the Israelites gathered together again. They read again from the book of the Law and spent time confessing their sin and worshiping God. The Levites told the people to stand and praise God. They said,

"Blessed be your glorious name, and may it be exalted above all blessing and praise. You alone are the LORD. You made the heavens, even the highest heavens, and all their starry host, the earth and all that is on it, the seas and all that is in them. You give life to everything, and the multitudes of heaven worship you.

"You are the LORD God, who chose Abram and brought him out of Ur of the Chaldeans and named him Abraham. You found his heart faithful to you, and you made a covenant with him to give to his descendants the land of the Canaanites, Hittites, Amorites, Perizzites, Jebusites and Girgashites. You have kept your promise because you are righteous.

"You saw the suffering of our forefathers in Egypt; you heard their cry at the Red Sea. You sent miraculous signs and wonders against Pharaoh, against all his officials and all the people of his land, for you know how arrogantly the Egyptians treated them. You made a name for yourself, which remains to this day. You divided the sea before them, so that they passed through it on dry ground, but you hurled their pursuers into the depths, like a stone into mighty waters.

By day you led them with a pillar of cloud, and by night with a pillar of fire to give them light on the way they were to take.

"You came down on Mount Sinai; you spoke to them from heaven. You gave them regulations and laws that are just and right, and decrees and commands that are good. You made known to them your holy Sabbath and gave them commands, decrees and laws through your servant Moses. In their hunger you gave them bread from heaven and in their thirst you brought them water from the rock; you told them to go in and take possession of the land you had sworn with uplifted hand to give them.

"But they, our forefathers, became arrogant and stiff-necked, and did not obey your commands. They refused to listen and failed to remember the miracles you performed among them. They became stiff-necked and in their rebellion appointed a leader in order to return to their slavery. But you are a forgiving God, gracious and compassionate, slow to anger and abounding in love. Therefore you did not desert them, even when they cast for themselves an image of a calf and said, 'This is your god, who brought you up out of Egypt,' or when they committed awful blasphemies.

"Because of your great compassion you did not abandon them in the desert. By day the pillar of cloud did not cease to guide them on their path, nor the pillar of fire by night to shine on the way they were to take. You gave your good Spirit to instruct them. You did not withhold your manna from their mouths, and you gave them water for their thirst. For forty years you sustained them in the desert; they lacked nothing, their clothes did not wear out nor did their feet become swollen.

"You gave them kingdoms and nations, allotting to them even the remotest frontiers. They took over the country of Sihon king of Heshbon and the country of Og king of Bashan. You made their sons as numerous as the stars in the sky, and you brought them into the land that you told their fathers to enter and possess. Their sons went in and took possession of the land. You subdued before them the Canaanites, who lived in the land; you handed the Canaanites over to them, along with their kings and the peoples of the land, to deal with them as they pleased. They captured fortified cities and fertile land; they took possession of houses filled with all kinds of good things, wells already dug, vineyards, olive groves and fruit trees in abundance. They ate to the full and were well-nourished; they reveled in your great goodness.

"But they were disobedient and rebelled against you; they put your law behind their backs. They killed your prophets, who had admonished them in order to turn them back to you; they committed awful blasphemies. So you handed them over to their enemies, who oppressed them. But when they were oppressed they cried out to you. From heaven you heard them, and in your great compassion you gave them deliverers, who rescued them from the hand of their enemies.

"But as soon as they were at rest, they again did what was evil in your sight. Then you abandoned them to the hand of their enemies so that they ruled over them. And when they cried out to you again, you heard from heaven, and in your compassion you delivered them time after time.

"You warned them to return to your law, but they became arrogant and disobeyed your commands. They sinned against your ordinances, by which a man will live if he obeys them. Stubbornly they turned their backs on you, became stiff-necked and refused to listen. For many years you were patient with them. By your Spirit you admonished them through your prophets. Yet they paid no attention, so you handed them over to the neighboring peoples. But in your great mercy you did not put an end to them or abandon them, for you are a gracious and merciful God.

"Now therefore, O our God, the great, mighty and awesome God, who keeps his covenant of love, do not let all this hardship seem trifling in your eyes—the hardship that has come upon us, upon our kings and leaders, upon our priests and prophets, upon our fathers and all your people, from the days of the kings of Assyria until today. In all that has happened to us, you have been just; you have acted faithfully, while we did wrong. Our kings, our leaders, our priests and our fathers did not follow your law; they did not pay attention to your commands or the warnings you gave them. Even while they were in their kingdom, enjoying your great goodness to them in the spacious and fertile land you gave them, they did not serve you or turn from their evil ways.

"But see, we are slaves today, slaves in the land you gave our forefathers so they could eat its fruit and the other good things it produces. Because of our sins, its abundant harvest goes to the kings you have placed over us. They rule over our bodies and our cattle as they please. We are in great distress."[207]

Then scripture says that in view of the things of which they had been reminded, the people committed to following God's law that Moses had delivered to the people. Remembering had led to obedience.

The Old Testament closes soon after the wall around Jerusalem was rebuilt. The New Testament opens with the good news that had been talked about in the Old Testament—the birth of Jesus Christ, the Son of God, the Messiah and Deliverer.

Jesus talked to people about the kingdom of God and about the life God wanted them to live. He told them what kind of heart God wanted his people to have. He referred often to the things that were said and done during the times of the Old Testament. He explained them in ways that challenged people's thinking and way of living, ways that helped people know God better. And Jesus lived a life that was and is an example for people to follow—a life that pleased God.

Jesus had followers who spent much time with him. He prepared them for the time when he would no longer be

[207] Nehemiah 9:5-37

121

with them. He prepared them to carry on God's work here on earth. Jesus said that he would not leave his disciples alone. He said that after he was gone God would send the Holy Spirit who would remind them of all Jesus had said to them and would teach them all things. Life for his disciples was not going to be easy and so, remembering what Jesus said would help them persevere in spite of the troubles they would face.

Jesus also told them that he would be crucified and buried but would rise from the dead. And just as he said, those things happened.

After rising from the dead, Jesus ascended into heaven and his disciples carried on the work for which Jesus had prepared them. And, true to his word, God sent the Holy Spirit to help them. On the day the Spirit was sent, the apostle Peter told the crowd that had gathered about Jesus. It was important to talk about the things Jesus had done, what was done to him and who he is. Peter said,

> "Men of Israel, listen to this: Jesus of Nazareth was a man accredited by God to you by miracles, wonders and signs, which God did among you through him, as you yourselves know. This man was handed over to you by God's set purpose and foreknowledge; and you, with the help of wicked men, put him to death by nailing him to the cross. But God raised him from the dead, freeing him from the agony of death, because it was impossible for death to keep its hold on him...God has raised this Jesus to life, and we are all witnesses of the fact. Exalted to the right hand of God, he has received from the Father the promised Holy Spirit and has poured out what you now see and hear...Therefore let all Israel be assured of this: God has made this Jesus,

whom you crucified, both Lord and Christ."[208]

The people were troubled at Peter's words and asked what they should do. Peter said,

> "Repent and be baptized, every one of you, in the name of Jesus Christ for the forgiveness of your sins. And you will receive the gift of the Holy Spirit. The promise is for you and your children and for all who are far off—for all whom the Lord our God will call."[209]

As in the Old Testament, hearing what God has done and what he wants results in obedience or disobedience. Knowing the story of Jesus called for a response to the good news Peter shared. That day many accepted Peter's message and were baptized. They became followers of Jesus.

Jesus' followers taught people about Jesus. They told his story again and again. And no matter how many times they talked about the gospel or good news about Jesus, they just kept on teaching.

It was still important to tell what God had done and was doing for his people. Jesus' life, death, burial, resurrection and ascension into heaven were now of utmost importance. Writing to the church in the city of Corinth, the apostle Paul said,

> "Now, brothers, I want to remind you of the gospel I preached to you, which you received and on which you have taken your stand. By this gospel you are saved, if you hold firmly to the word I preached to you.

[208] Acts 2:22-24, 32-33, 36
[209] Acts 2:38-39

Otherwise, you have believed in vain. For what I received I passed on to you as of first importance: that Christ died for our sins according to the Scriptures, that he was buried, that he was raised on the third day according to the Scriptures, and that he appeared to Peter, and then to the Twelve. After that, he appeared to more than five hundred of the brothers at the same time, most of whom are still living, though some have fallen asleep. Then he appeared to James, then to all the apostles, and last of all he appeared to me also, as to one abnormally born."[210]

After Jesus had returned to heaven, his followers had begun spreading the good news about him and what God had done through him. As they did so, opposition against them and the church increased. Jesus' followers were often arrested and beaten. Stephen, a follower who was full of God's grace and power, was arrested and taken before the Sanhedrin, a council of Jews that was given some authority by the Roman government. Stephen spoke, as he had been doing, with wisdom and by the Holy Spirit.[211] When asked if the charges against him were true, Stephen gave the following answer:

"Brothers and fathers, listen to me! The God of glory appeared to our father Abraham while he was still in Mesopotamia, before he lived in Haran. 'Leave your country and your people,' God said, 'and go to the land I will show you.'

"So he left the land of the Chaldeans and settled in Haran. After the death of his father, God sent him to this land where you

[210] 1 Corinthians 15:1-8
[211] Acts 6:9-10

are now living. He gave him no inheritance here, not even a foot of ground. But God promised him that he and his descendants after him would possess the land, even though at that time Abraham had no child. God spoke to him in this way: 'Your descendants will be strangers in a country not their own, and they will be enslaved and mistreated four hundred years. But I will punish the nation they serve as slaves,' God said, 'and afterward they will come out of that country and worship me in this place.' Then he gave Abraham the covenant of circumcision. And Abraham became the father of Isaac and circumcised him eight days after his birth. Later Isaac became the father of Jacob, and Jacob became the father of the twelve patriarchs.

"Because the patriarchs were jealous of Joseph, they sold him as a slave into Egypt. But God was with him and rescued him from all his troubles. He gave Joseph wisdom and enabled him to gain the goodwill of Pharaoh king of Egypt; so he made him ruler over Egypt and all his palace.

"Then a famine struck all Egypt and Canaan, bringing great suffering, and our fathers could not find food. When Jacob heard that there was grain in Egypt, he sent our fathers on their first visit. On their second visit, Joseph told his brothers who he was, and Pharaoh learned about Joseph's family. After this, Joseph sent for his father Jacob and his whole family, seventy-five in all. Then Jacob went down to Egypt, where he and our fathers died. Their bodies were brought back to Shechem and placed in the tomb that Abraham had bought from the sons of Hamor at Shechem for a certain sum of money.

"As the time drew near for God to fulfill his promise to Abraham, the number of our people in Egypt greatly increased. Then another king, who knew nothing about Joseph, became ruler of Egypt. He dealt treacherously with our people and oppressed our forefathers by forcing them to throw out their newborn babies so that they would die.

"At that time Moses was born, and he was no ordinary child. For three months he was cared for in his father's house. When he was placed outside, Pharaoh's daughter took him and brought him up as her own son. Moses was educated in all the wisdom of the Egyptians and was powerful in speech and action.

"When Moses was forty years old, he decided to visit his fellow Israelites. He saw one of them being mistreated by an Egyptian, so he went to his defense and avenged him by killing the Egyptian. Moses thought that his own people would realize that God was using him to rescue them, but they did not. The next day Moses came upon two Israelites who were fighting. He tried to reconcile them by saying, 'Men, you are brothers; why do you want to hurt each other?'

"But the man who was mistreating the other pushed Moses aside and said, 'Who made you ruler and judge over us? Do you want to kill me as you killed the Egyptian yesterday?' When Moses heard this, he fled to Midian, where he settled as a foreigner and had two sons.

"After forty years had passed, an angel appeared to Moses in the flames of a burning bush in the desert near Mount Sinai. When he saw this, he was amazed at the sight. As he went over to look more closely, he heard the Lord's voice: 'I am the God of your fathers, the God of Abraham, Isaac and Jacob.' Moses trembled with fear and did not dare to look.

"Then the Lord said to him, 'Take off your sandals; the place where you are standing is holy ground. I have indeed seen the oppression of my people in Egypt. I have heard their groaning and have come down to set them free. Now come, I will send you back to Egypt.'

"This is the same Moses whom they had rejected with the words, 'Who made you ruler and judge?' He was sent to be their ruler and deliverer by God himself, through the angel who appeared to him in the bush. He led them out of Egypt and did wonders and miraculous signs in Egypt, at the Red Sea and for forty years in the desert.

"This is that Moses who told the Israelites, 'God will send you a prophet like me from your own people.' He was in the assembly in the desert, with the angel who spoke to him on Mount Sinai, and with our fathers; and he received living words to pass on to us.

"But our fathers refused to obey him. Instead, they rejected him and in their hearts turned back to Egypt. They told Aaron, 'Make us gods who will go before us. As for this fellow Moses who led us out of Egypt—we don't know what has happened to him!' That was the time they made an idol in the form of a calf. They brought sacrifices to it and held a celebration in honor of what their hands had made. But God turned away and gave them over to the worship of the heavenly bodies. This agrees with what is written in the book of the prophets: 'Did you bring me sacrifices and offerings forty years in the desert, O house of Israel? You have lifted up the shrine of Molech and the star of your god Rephan, the idols you made to worship. Therefore I will send you into exile' beyond Babylon.

"Our forefathers had the tabernacle of the Testimony with them in the desert. It had been made as God directed Moses, according to the pattern he had seen. Having received the tabernacle, our fathers under Joshua brought it with them when they took the land from the nations God drove out before them. It remained in the land until the time of David, who enjoyed God's favor and asked that he might provide a dwelling place for the God of Jacob. But it was Solomon who built the house for him.

"However, the Most High does not live in houses made by men. As the prophet says: 'Heaven is my throne, and the earth is my footstool. What kind of house will you build for me? says the Lord. Or where will my resting place be? Has not my hand made all these things?'

"You stiff-necked people, with uncircumcised hearts and ears! You are just like your fathers: You always resist the Holy Spirit! Was there ever a prophet your fathers did not persecute? They even killed those who predicted the coming of the Righteous One. And now you have betrayed and murdered him—you who have received the law that was put into effect through angels but have not obeyed it."[212]

Stephen had reminded them of the things God had done and what had happened to God's people down through the ages. He talked about Abraham, Isaac, Jacob, Jacob's twelve sons, including Joseph, and then about Moses. He talked about the killing of God's prophets and, finally, the killing of the Righteous One, Jesus.

Afterwards, the people were furious and, dragging Stephen out of the city, they stoned him to death. "On that day a great persecution broke out against the church at Jerusalem, and all except the apostles were scattered throughout Judea and Samaria."[213] Despite the increased persecution and imprisonment of Jesus' followers, they continued to tell the story of Jesus and what his life, death, burial, resurrection and ascension into heaven meant for people. And they continued to tell it in the context of what God had been doing for ages among his people.

A young Jewish man named Saul was present when Stephen was stoned. After Stephen's death, Saul worked very zealously to destroy the church. He had many believers arrested and thrown into prison. After awhile, Jesus spoke to Saul, and he became convinced of who

[212] Acts 7:2-53
[213] Acts 8:1

Jesus is. He believed that Jesus is the Son of God. And Saul began to preach. Using God's word in the Old Testament, he proved that Jesus is the Christ or the Messiah that God had been promising to send.

Later, Saul, also called Paul, was asked to speak before a group of people. He told them the story of what God had done for his people. He said,

> "Men of Israel and you Gentiles who worship God, listen to me! The God of the people of Israel chose our fathers; he made the people prosper during their stay in Egypt, with mighty power he led them out of that country, he endured their conduct for about forty years in the desert, he overthrew seven nations in Canaan and gave their land to his people as their inheritance. All this took about 450 years.

> "After this, God gave them judges until the time of Samuel the prophet. Then the people asked for a king, and he gave them Saul son of Kish, of the tribe of Benjamin, who ruled forty years. After removing Saul, he made David their king. He testified concerning him: 'I have found David son of Jesse a man after my own heart; he will do everything I want him to do.'

> "From this man's descendants God has brought to Israel the Savior Jesus, as he promised. Before the coming of Jesus, John preached repentance and baptism to all the people of Israel. As John was completing his work, he said: 'Who do you think I am? I am not that one. No, but he is coming after me, whose sandals I am not worthy to untie.'

"Brothers, children of Abraham, and you God-fearing Gentiles, it is to us that this message of salvation has been sent. The people of Jerusalem and their rulers did not recognize Jesus, yet in condemning him they fulfilled the words of the prophets that are read every Sabbath. Though they found no proper ground for a death sentence, they asked Pilate to have him executed. When they had carried out all that was written about him, they took him down from the tree and laid him in a tomb. But God raised him from the dead, and for many days he was seen by those who had traveled with him from Galilee to Jerusalem. They are now his witnesses to our people.

"We tell you the good news: What God promised our fathers he has fulfilled for us, their children, by raising up Jesus. As it is written in the second Psalm: 'You are my Son; today I have become your Father.' The fact that God raised him from the dead, never to decay, is stated in these words: 'I will give you the holy and sure blessings promised to David.' So it is stated elsewhere: 'You will not let your Holy One see decay.'

"For when David had served God's purpose in his own generation, he fell asleep; he was buried with his fathers and his body decayed. But the one whom God raised from the dead did not see decay.

"Therefore, my brothers, I want you to know that through Jesus the forgiveness of sins is proclaimed to you. Through him everyone who believes is justified from everything you could not be justified from by the law of Moses."[214]

When Paul wrote to the church in Philippi, he told them, "It is no trouble for me to write the same things to you again, and it is a safeguard for you."[215] He went on to warn them about false teachers and putting confidence in outward things.

The apostle Peter wrote to a group of Christians about how to be effective and productive in their knowledge of Jesus. He wanted them to never fall, but to receive a rich welcome into Jesus' eternal kingdom, so he wrote to them,

> "... I will always remind you of these things, even though you know them and are firmly established in the truth you now have. I think it is right to refresh your memory as long as I live in the tent of this body... And I will make every effort to see that after my departure you will always be able to remember these things."[216]

It always has been and still is important to remember the story of what God has done and continues to do for his people. May we say as David did so long ago,

> "I will exalt you, my God the King; I will praise your name for ever and ever. Every day I will praise you and extol your name for ever and ever. Great is the LORD and most worthy of praise; his greatness no one can fathom. One generation will commend your works to another; they will tell of your mighty acts. They will speak of the glorious

[214] Acts 13:16-39
[215] Philippians 3:1
[216] 2 Peter 1:12-13, 15

splendor of your majesty, and I will meditate on your wonderful works. They will tell of the power of your awesome works, and I will proclaim your great deeds. They will celebrate your abundant goodness and joyfully sing of your righteousness."[217]

And may we, as David did, say to God,

"I meditate on all your works and consider what your hands have done. I spread out my hands to you; my soul thirsts for you like a parched land."[218]

God is still very active in the lives of his people, individually and collectively. He continues to do wonderful and awesome deeds. It is just as important today as ever before to remember, to speak of and to meditate on those deeds, and not only those from ages past, but what he is doing now in and among his people. Doing that can help us find reassurance, comfort, encouragement and rest for our souls. It can remind us of God's zealous love and his faithfulness to his people—to each of us. It can remind us of God's power and of his creativity in accomplishing his will. It can help us remember how badly he wants to be in a relationship with us. It can help us persevere, walk faithfully and hold fast to our God as we remember his promises and what he has done for us personally. It is a good way to be challenged in our walk with him, and it can keep hope ever before us. When we speak of and meditate on what God has been and is doing, we keep the story of our God alive in our hearts and minds.

[217] Psalm 145:1-7
[218] Psalm 143:5-6

Questions for Thought

What are some mighty works you have seen God do?

What can you do to keep the story of God alive in your heart and mind? What are the benefits of doing that?

WHAT DOES THIS HAVE TO DO WITH ME?

Here I am at the end of this book. I've had fun writing it, and I hope you've enjoyed the "story"—the true story of an awesome, magnificent and loving God!

I feel very blessed to live in a time and place that allows me the privilege of owning a copy of God's word, the Bible. Actually, I own several copies. Reading them, I've discovered that God makes the most important things very clear to us. He does that through repetition, the wording he uses, the use of word pictures, giving examples, providing application, telling stories and much more.

When I think about reading the Bible, many things come to mind. First and foremost is how God reveals himself to us through it. He shows what he is like as he speaks to and interacts with people in both the Old and New Testaments. He also reveals himself through the life and words of Jesus. Jesus did nothing apart from God. The Bible teaches that if we know Jesus we know the Father who sent him. We also learn about him from the New Testament writings as they provide descriptions of God and tell about what he wants for us.

God reveals his passionate and immeasurable love for us through his Word. When I open my Bible to read or study what God has said, I am usually overwhelmed with the love I see communicated in it. In so many ways God demonstrates and describes his love. He tells us again and again the things he wants us to know about that love. I've learned to look for that every time I open my Bible. I do find it, and I cherish it. As I grow in Jesus, I understand more and more about his love for me. And I realize that I barely begin to fathom the nature and extent of that love. I know for certain, though, that his love for me will never fail.

In the Bible, God also reveals his will for us. He tells us to learn what is pleasing to him, and in the Bible he demonstrates and explains what that is. We learn from his commands and from the examples of Jesus and others who lived godly lives—lives that pleased God. He also says he wants all people to be saved—to not have to pay for or be punished for our sins—and he tells us how he has provided for that. God enables us to be and do all that he has called us to be and do. He graciously provides the Holy Spirit to help us in many ways.

God's will for me is that I might live in a loving and obedient relationship with him. Jesus lived and died so that our sins could be forgiven and that we might have the hope of living with God forever. He tells us that when Jesus was raised from the dead and went back into heaven, the Holy Spirit was sent to the earth. When we are baptized into Jesus we receive the gift of his Holy Spirit. His Spirit lives within those who give their lives to Jesus. God never leaves us alone but is always with us. He is a loving and faithful God, a God who is very passionate about his people. He himself is our strength and our salvation. And his will for us after this earthly life is that we live an eternity in the glorious presence of our God and Savior.

When I read God's Word, I am challenged to grow as a person and become more like God and Jesus. I am challenged, strengthened, encouraged and comforted in my relationship with him as I come to know him better and move closer and closer to the heart of God.

Knowing God gives me a reason to face each day with a sense of purpose, expectation and abundant joy. It allows me to give of my time and myself to others. God provides me with a confidence and faith that comes from knowing who he is, that he is with me, that he knows best what I need and that he has the power to bring about his will in my life. Knowing God has provided a peace that I never knew existed, a wholeness greater than anything I could ever imagine and an awareness of being loved that surrounds my whole being. Knowing God and feasting on his word has resulted in a hope that can withstand whatever I might face. I can't do that on my own; it only happens by God's power and love.

That all sounds very rosy. I'll tell you, though, that he and his Word have carried me through times of disappointment, confusion, anger, illness and grieving. At times he has lifted me up out of an ocean full of tears. He has provided people to walk with me on my sometimes difficult, sometimes fun journey through life. He has healed hurts that I thought would never heal.

The Bible promises in James 4:8, "Come near to God and he will come near to you." Also, Jesus said he came so we would have a full and abundant life. I believe both of these are true and, in fact, have experienced both of them.

I believe God celebrates with me the victory I find in him each day as well as the victory to which I look forward when my earthly life ends. He celebrates with me accomplishments, answered prayers, the light at the end of the tunnel, big and small joys. I believe he celebrates with me the completion of this book.

I encourage you to delve into the Bible and find for yourself the things I have found and much more.

Made in the USA
Coppell, TX
24 January 2022

72219541R00090